COME INTO MY OFFICE

COME INTO MY OFFICE

STORIES FROM AN HR LEADER IN SILICON VALLEY

BY MAI TON

NEW DEGREE PRESS

COME INTO MY OFFICE

Stories from an HR Leader in Silicon Valley

ISBN   978-1-63676-860-1 *Paperback*

        978-1-63730-182-1 *Kindle Ebook*

        978-1-63730-304-7 *Ebook*

To my mother, Hien Nguyen, my sister, Amanda Ton, and my daughter, Emma Pai: The three most powerful forces in my life.

CONTENTS

————

It is not the most intellectual of the species that survives; it is not the strongest that survives; but the species that survives is the one that is able best to adapt and adjust to the changing environment in which it finds itself.

—CHARLES DARWIN, ON THE ORIGIN OF SPECIES

FOREWORD BY EMMA PAI

Emma, the author's daughter at 12 years old

From the day I entered this world, my mom has been telling me stories about how she is the only woman on her executive team. She is a very talented, hardworking mom and deserves so much more credit than she gets. Being the only woman on her team must be hard, not that I would know, though. I'm only twelve years old. When I was six years old, I remember thinking that my mom didn't fit in, but that's not her fault. Why does the work world contain so many men? Is it always going to be like this? I hope it's not like this when I grow up and start working.

When I was younger, my mom would travel around the world for her work. Sometimes she would bring me along. Those times were always really fun for me because I got to travel to different places, meet new people, and try different foods from around the world. My mom and I made it a tradition to have afternoon tea in London. That was my favorite thing to do with her on our London trips. It was always super fun to talk and laugh over tea. I'm glad that my mom wrote this book to display what she does and how hard she works.

I remember how my mom would spend time shopping with me in cities like London and Paris. Somehow, she would always pick out these stunning outfits for me. That's probably why I'm so into fashion. She shared many stories about her work with me. I just hope one day that I find a job that makes me happy like my mom's job did for her.

For the past few years, I have been watching my mom sit at her desk with her laptop writing this book. It was always her excuse out of doing things, so I'm just glad we're done with it. It has sucked so much time out of her life, but I'm so proud of her for finally finishing it. I'm only twelve years old, so I don't know what I want to be or do when I grow up, but I do know that I want to be just as dedicated and committed as my mom. She has always made time for me (even though she has been writing this book for so many years); she has always been there. At least it has felt like that.

Looking back, I have realized that there's no specific way I have to live my life. Just look at my mom. She is always doing her own thing and is her own individual self. I want to live up to her expectations and live the same life she did—obviously not the exact same but pretty similar. I hope that my mom keeps the same bubbly personality and colorful inside. It's so exciting to look at this amazing, bright, cheerful, driven figure and be able to say "that's my mom." She is such a great example and influence. A lot of people I know look up to her, including myself. Of course, she can be really annoying and weird sometimes, but I still love her. She has always been committed and dedicated, yet I didn't realize this until now. I am so grateful to have such a loving and caring mom. I hope you enjoy her book. It took her a long time to write it!

INTRODUCTION

———

In 2015, my daughter taught me a lesson I'll never forget. At the time, I was working as the vice president of human resources at a tech start-up in San Francisco. My daughter Emma, then only seven years old, wandered into my office one day, picked up a photo from my desk, and stared at it, confused. "Mommy, why do you work with a bunch of men?"

I looked over her shoulder and studied the photo, seeing it—for the first time—through new eyes. There I was, on stage with my executive team, surrounded by a sea of White men. My small frame was almost swallowed by their towering figures, my tan skin and dark hair contrasting heavily against their white button-down shirts. At that moment, I realized that this had been my reality for as long as I could remember; I was so used to blending in that I never realized how much I stood out.

A window into my professional life

How long had things been like this?

I always knew I sat among talented folks, but I failed to realize that none of them acted or looked like me. While being the "only" at the table was once a source of pride for me, I suddenly began to see my experiences in a new light. I began to feel very lonely and isolated being the only woman and only minority at the executive table.

For instance, I was one of the few executives who found it odd that the jokes told around the executive table were sworn to secrecy because they were not appropriate for any room except the one where all of these men sat together. Giving women nicknames, assigning initials for hard-to-pronounce names, or even mistaking one person for another showed the lack of regard that was present throughout my career in tech start-ups.

These days, discrimination and dysfunction at work happen very subtly. Gone are the days of *overt* racism or *overt* sexual harassment in the workplace, making it hard to pinpoint when our coworkers are acting like jerks. It becomes even harder to call out leaders for their unprofessional behavior when the moments happen quickly and subtly.

Many coworkers can be problematic if they are left to their own devices. Sometimes they can't help themselves because they are not aware of how the jokes, nicknames, or mistakes hurt their own colleagues. Since we are forced to work with these types of people—and I believe every company has some version of this type of person—the motley crew of colleagues that surround you every day shape who you are too.

This motley crew of work colleagues reminds me of the American holiday of Thanksgiving: Each year, we sit around a table eating a wonderful feast with some family and some collection of friends. We chat about all the things for which we are grateful with people that we sometimes have just met that same day. The cast of characters around the table changes every year, yet we endure lively discussions as if we've been family and friends forever.

While Thanksgiving comes around just once a year, I think its spirit lives in the workplace each day. Think about it: for eight plus hours a day, for almost 365 days a year, we're crammed inside an office with our coworkers, some of whom we'd prefer not to associate with if we could help it. We're forced to laugh at awkward jokes, respond to messages, and work alongside them, and we barely know them.

The conversations and situations at work force us to engage in dialogues with people with whom we have nothing in common. These colleagues come from different places with many beliefs disparate from our own. Are these the people we'd choose to sit with? Probably not, and still, we all have to pretend that we enjoy each other's company and work on the same team with no escape except to the bathrooms and our own occasional vacations and holidays. Work becomes very complicated when you are forced to confront these differences with people we would normally not associate with.

I once called out an executive for using too many curse words, and he didn't take it well. "Gary, I would appreciate it if you could limit the number of curse words you use when talking at all-hands meetings. You are more than Gary here; you are a C-level leader, and what you say gets mimicked in the workplace. I don't want this place to become what I think could be a male-centric or a "bro"-ish environment." The next day I got an earful from him about how he had made millions and took this start-up job almost out of pity, and who was I to tell him that he shouldn't curse? It was a heated exchange—one that still haunts me because all I asked him to do was limit his curse words. As a human resources (HR) leader, I have witnessed and facilitated resolutions for many interoffice conflicts. Some ended well, while others made me question my own efficacy, even when I knew it was the right conversation.

The role of an HR leader at a start-up covers a wide berth. We are responsible for managing the people strategy of the business, which is one of the most unpredictable pieces of the puzzle to maneuver. Employees come and go for a multitude of reasons, and you must constantly adapt to a casting change *each week*. Couple that with many changing business priorities, and the puzzle gets more complicated as the days go by.

The pressure to move fast and work with many people not from your "tribe" makes the work environment stressful and full of tension. Unhealthy work environments make us unhealthy ourselves. In this knowledge- and service-based economy, we are arguably more depressed, suicidal, and unhealthy than at any other point in history. Researchers published in the *International Journal on Disability and*

Human Development call these unhealthy factors "life-threatening stressors."[1]

As the HR leader for six different tech start-ups, I've been the one that called bullsh*t on coworkers who told racist and misogynistic jokes while others remained silent and complicit. All this responsibility often made me feel like I was the only adult in the room, in addition to sometimes being the only woman and minority at the executive table. *Where was everyone else's moral compass? Was I the only one who had turned mine on each day?*

After Emma pointed out the photo on my desk, I promised myself that I would do everything in my power to make the world of tech feel less lonely for other children dreaming of working in Silicon Valley. I had my work cut out for me.

For the past fifteen years, in every company I worked for, I introduced all sorts of leadership classes designed to uncover our natural inherent biases. I was looking for microaggressions. The Merriam–Webster dictionary defines microaggression as "a comment or action that subtly and often unconsciously or unintentionally expresses a prejudiced attitude toward a member of a marginalized group (such as a racial minority)[2]". I found plenty of these instances in my daily work.

I read through every performance review, and I found words that characterized men as passionate leaders while women were viewed as emotional. I reviewed promotion

---

1 Jong-Min Woo and Teodor T. Postolache, "The Impact of Work Environment on Mood Disorders and Suicide: Evidence and Implications," *International Journal on Disability and Human Development 7, no. 2* (2008): 185-200.

2 *Merriam-Webster, s.v. "microaggression (n.)," accessed March 14, 2021.*

processes to ensure women and men and minorities and nonminorities were being promoted at the same rates, which meant I read every single word of every single review to understand whether our managers applied the criteria we created for promotions equally across genders and ethnicities. I looked at the language we used on our corporate websites to check for any gender-biased words (ninja, pinch hitter, A-player, etc.) and changed what I could to represent a more open and inclusive company. I wish I could provide a playbook for how to tackle these microaggressions; what I committed to doing was to write about these examples in this book to encourage you to reflect on how you—how *we all*—play a role in making our work environments more stressful than necessary. We need to serve as better examples for the future generations coming into the workforce.

I spent many years reminding people to be more thoughtful about their actions and words. I hosted trainings and booked one-on-one meetings to give specific coaching to leaders; I even hired executive coaches for leaders to tackle some of these subtle workplace situations. Nothing changed, and all these efforts didn't seem to yield the fruit I planted. I felt like Sisyphus rolling the boulder up the hill only for it to land on me.

What was I doing wrong? Why couldn't I fix this?

Then it hit me.

All these years, I had been the only one doing the work.

Looking back, I realize that having the sole responsibility of calling out the sexist jokes or the inappropriate comments said out loud by coworkers who claimed innocence is what made me burn out. The emotional toll of years of hard, high-effort work to get employees to behave like adults in the workplace had been exhausting. It was too big of a burden for any one person to have to carry alone.

Being the "only" at the table wasn't the problem. I was a professional, and I held my own in every office I worked in, but being the only one doing the work to improve our office behavior is what ultimately got to me. If just one more person had been on my side, perhaps that proverbial boulder would have been pushed over the hill instead of crushing me on its way back down.

Colleagues fighting and arguing with each other made me think that they were losing sight of the fact that the enemy was always outside of the walls of the business—the competition. They were colleagues on the same team known as work. Somehow many people lose sight of this and become vicious to each other, and many others spend a ton of mental gymnastics trying to get along. It made me frustrated and sad that colleagues became counterproductive with each other. If they would have stopped to look around, they would have noticed that the train wreck happened many stops ago.

Everyone has the power to call out anyone who crosses the line of professionalism. Each person, no matter their role, shares equal responsibility for carrying the weight of this work. Women and people of color may never feel safe doing this in the workplace if they don't see their coworkers engaged in this work with them. I was the only one in some of these rooms of privilege that took the time to deliver feedback and call out bullsh*t, and it wasn't just because of my role; it was because I knew it was wrong. I had to fight this battle for my daughter and for future generations in the workplace. I wanted to demand better. It was a lonely and exhausting part of my workload, and it wore me out. Ultimately, all the -*ist* (racist, sexist, etc.) behaviors at work inspired me to write this book.

My experiences have helped me see that lasting change can only be created when everyone does their part to shape their workplace to make it safe for everyone. Be an ally, be compassionate, and be kind to each other. The hours we spend together as working adults are the hours that we spend away from our family and friends, and I strove (and still strive) to make work worth the sacrifice. Bullying, teasing, name-calling, and any type of statements that demean your own colleagues should not be accepted in the places we call work.

I encourage readers to step up and call out racism, sexism, or inappropriate behaviors whenever you see them—in your personal lives but especially in your professional lives. I urge every reader to take action and call out behaviors at work that don't fit the culture of the workplace you call home for eight hours per day, five days per week. If we all take responsibility, then the burden won't rest solely and crushingly on the shoulders of single individuals in HR, such as myself.

In this book, which is part memoir, I will showcase stories that will take you inside the tech industry, showing the "real" everyday stories that you won't get from media. Written from my perspective as an HR leader with insider information behind the scenes of various top-level decisions, I will unveil moments of real chaos. While conducting my research and interviews with other HR leaders, I learned that the unbelievable moments I experienced were indeed commonplace. I decided to tell these stories raw and (relatively) uncensored* in the hopes of making the tech industry a better place for everybody.

Silicon Valley calls them People teams but for purposes of this book, I will use human resources or HR since the world is more familiar with that term.

*Please note: I changed the names and scrambled some of the events and dates to protect my beloved colleagues.

PART 1

LOVE TO HATE

CHAPTER 1

BEGINNINGS

———

When I graduated from college with my newly minted sociology degree, I wanted to change the world. I was young and eager, and I vowed to find a profession where I could make a difference. I wanted to change the world and make it more equal for underprivileged people who did not have the luck I did to attend college. After graduating, it took me two months to find a job where I thought I could do so. I became a social worker.

MY LIFE AS A SOCIAL WORKER

The realities of the uphill battle that many poor people face revealed themselves to me after just three months in my career as a social worker. For one full year, I went through an extensive state-sponsored training program to help poor families qualify for food stamps and Aid to Families with Dependent Children (AFDC)—two programs that provided free services to families in underserved communities. We had real-life cases during the training program that brought me to tears almost every day. These welfare programs helped put food on tables, made sure families had healthcare, and gave adults resources and training to find jobs to stabilize their families. The intent of these social programs was to eventually elevate these poor families out of these temporary social programs. Instead, I witnessed that my clients were "lifers" in these programs in that they relied on these systems so heavily that they had a hard time finding their way out of them.[3]

My days as a newly trained social worker consisted of eight appointments where I would interview the families, collect certain data, and determine if they were eligible for free social services like food stamps and AFDC. Sometimes, whole families would show up and cram into my windowless office to emphasize the magnitude of their families and how dependent they were on these free programs. They were trying to escape the cycles of poverty that had gripped their families for too long.

I'll never forget Darryl Phillips, one of my clients at that time. He was merely seventeen years old, went to school off and on, and had a steady girlfriend. One day, he came into the building and asked at the front desk to see me. For most social workers, their days are packed back-to-back with appointments that are typically booked months in advance. It was abnormal to pop in and see your social worker. Since it seemed urgent, I let the guards know that I was available to see Darryl. I assumed it must be some sort of good news for him to drop by my office in person like this.

I didn't want the conversation to last for too long, so I remained standing as Darryl came into my small office in downtown Houston. "I have some really important news that I wanted to tell you in person, Ms. Mai." He was the only client who called me by my first name.

---

3   USA.gov, "Government Benefits," accessed February 21, 2021.

I smiled and told him I was excited to hear it.

He took a deep breath: "Ms. Mai, my girlfriend is pregnant, and I'm so excited to become a daddy. It's been a dream of mine for a long time!"

I looked at him in shock and disbelief and sat down. I couldn't handle the weight of what he told me. Here I was, a young college graduate hoping to change the world by breaking the cycle of poverty. Here Darryl was telling me that he wanted to be a father when he was barely an adult himself.

I don't remember exactly what I said, but I'm pretty sure I didn't congratulate him. Instead, I asked, "Are you going to stay in school, and how are you going to support your new family?" I'm sure I took the wind out of his sails. I couldn't believe that Darryl was excited to become a father when I couldn't see how he was going to be successful without taking care of *himself* first.

That was the day I said that I couldn't stay in social work. How was Darryl going to support a family without a high school education, a job, or even a plan? In that moment, I realized that I had a life of privilege coming out of college, landing a job, and earning a steady income. I couldn't imagine what it felt like for Darryl who didn't have that fortune. I could not solve the pieces of the puzzle to help Darryl. He needed someone to mentor him and guide him, which couldn't be me because I didn't know how to be helpful.

Some might say I gave up on people that I should have supported. To them I say, I learned very quickly that the world isn't all rainbows and glitter like I thought. I was on my own journey to discover who I was, what I cared about, and what I could do to change all the bad luck that made life tough for so many underprivileged and poor people throughout the country.

It makes me wonder where Darryl is today and whatever became of him. My intent was always to be helpful to people in need, but as a young college graduate, I could not figure out how to break a pattern of generational poverty.

This experience of working in social work quickly dampened my idealistic dreams of developing a more equitable and kind society.

According to the Urban Institute, the United States' spending for public welfare programs in one year, totals more than $673 billion, which represents 22 percent of the general budget.[4] This figure identifies the mounting price tag we must afford to help those that need these programs the most. During my time as a social worker, I had no idea that so many people needed help. I was determined to find work that would make me wealthy enough to help whoever I could so that they would never have to go on a government-sponsored welfare program. This was the first time that I thought about money and how I was going to make any with my liberal arts degree.

Darryl must have felt alone and isolated. I did too. How was I going to help people when I didn't have enough experience in the real world?

As I looked for my next job, I swung from the direction of more altruistic tendencies and toward the ability to make a lot of money. I tried my hand at a myriad of other jobs to find my true passion. I served as a claims adjuster for an insurance company, a telemarketer, a market research coordinator, and a recruiter. Despite trying on so many different jobs, and after all those experiences, I felt I still hadn't found my true passion. I had career switches associated typically with the

---

4   Urban Institute, "State and Local Finance Initiative," 2011.

millennial generation. According to a study by EdSurge, an award-winning education news organization, "Millennials will change jobs an average of four times in their first decade out of college, compared to about two job changes by Gen Xers their first ten years out of college." [5]. I was a Gen Xer acting like a millennial.

MY DAYS IN INVESTMENT BANKING

As I was feeling lost, one day out of the blue, a recruiter sent me an email about a position at an investment bank. I knew no one who worked in investment banking at the time, but it sounded sexy. I had only heard about the lives of bankers who traveled globally, went out to events, and wined and dined for a living while transacting huge business deals over those dinners. Since I hadn't found my true passion yet, I thought I would take a chance on something new again. I anticipated earning a nice living from the fat bonus checks that came with working in banking. I went for the interview and got the job! They offered me a job as a research assistant in the healthcare division of the bank. I would be working with a bunch of Ivy League-educated bankers and their staff on the biggest healthcare deals of my life—right out of Silicon Valley. The three-hour time difference between San Francisco and New York, the mecca of the US stock market and *the* banking center of the United States, meant we started our days at 7:30 a.m. PT and ended our days at 3:30 p.m. PT—not the best timing for trying to have a social life.

---

5   Jeffery R. Young, "How Many Times Will People Change Jobs? The Myth of the Endlessly-Job-Hopping Millennial," EdSurge, July 20, 2017.

It was a new world for me, and I thought I could make a lot of money and retire early like so many other investment bankers I grew to know.

The first few months were overwhelming. I didn't know what I was doing, so I did whatever they told me to do. I worked with three bankers, and they had me busy all day long. Some days were spent doing research on the internet about various companies and individuals, while other days were spent creating PowerPoint decks that captured tons of data points on the market value of a potential merger between two companies. Some of the decks we created were one hundred pages long and were never used since the deals never came to fruition.

The work was intense, and the people I worked with sacrificed their personal lives for the potential of financial rewards from handling these multimillion-dollar transactions. With the long hours and grueling travel schedules, people who worked in this field never seemed to have time to be with friends and family. One of the bankers I worked with didn't even make it to the birth of his first child, having spent sixteen hours in the office that particular day. He took a taxi to the hospital *after* his child was born.

As I became more acquainted with my colleagues, I realized that many of them went to prestigious Ivy League universities for both their undergraduate and graduate degrees. "Why do we ONLY recruit from Ivy League universities?" I asked our recruiting leader at the time.

She responded, "We've been really successful getting English and history majors to join our junior teams, so we figured out our sweet spot-on specific campuses."

I always wondered how Abby, who had a degree in 1865–1900 English literature, chose to work in investment banking.

She said, "My English degree helps me communicate with these sophisticated business leaders in multinational companies." I thought the answer was a bit elitist, but I was glad Abby could put such a specific degree to work in the real world.

Lunches would be ordered in every day, and the bankers ate like crap. They ate whatever they wanted and didn't care. Some of them had Pepto-Bismol on their desks as if it was an accessory. They took swigs of the pink liquid straight from the bottle at all moments of the day. I watched them drink from those bottles as if they were drinking water.

Divorces were commonplace, and affairs with colleagues and drugs filled the rumor mills in our department almost weekly. This was not the life I wanted to live, even if I was only tangentially involved in these sexy multimillion dollar deals. The job paid me a ton of money, but at the end of the day, the work wasn't for me. The stress began to eat away at me. I spent my peaceful twenty-minute walking commute praying that everything would go smoothly for that day. It was an unhealthy working environment.

I watched people get yelled and screamed at daily. One time, I actually found drugs in the bathroom, and I didn't know what to do, so I left the tiny bag on the counter. The stress and pressure made people lose their marbles. Throwing things at each other, firing people on the spot—I had never seen such unprofessional behavior in the workplace. I didn't know if this behavior was normal. Earning obscene amounts of money must have driven people to absorb the abuse and stick around.

After six months on the job, things inevitably turned south for me. I became the recipient of a tirade from one of the bankers I worked with.

As their stress levels climbed, the bankers I worked with started assigning me crazy-difficult tasks with near-impossible deadlines. They yelled at me for any simple mistake or error, never tolerating any excuses. They demanded a level of perfection that I could not maintain because I barely understood what they did with all the sophisticated transactions.

The day I got a tongue-lashing from my main banker was the day I decided I needed a new job. I had accidentally faxed (it was the 1990s, so faxes were a quick dial-up way to communicate) a sheet which offered deal terms for a potential merger and acquisition (M&A) between two big healthcare companies. The fax cover sheet and term sheet were left on my desk with a fax number written on a sticky note. I wanted to be proactive and faxed the sheet over to the client. I left the fax confirmation sheet on my banker's desk.

When Brent got out of his meeting, he immediately came out of his corner office and yelled, "Mai, what the hell did you do?" I could see that he was holding the fax confirmation sheet.

"I faxed the term sheet you left on my desk. I thought you wanted me to send it over," I said sheepishly.

Brent screamed, "You know what happens when you assume, right? You make an ass out of both of us."

I held back my tears and shot back, "Then why did you leave the term sheet with a fax cover sheet and a fax number on my desk?"

Brent snapped, "Mai, this was a deal that would net out millions of dollars for one of the CEOs listed, and I wanted to show him the numbers. Now because you sent that term sheet out, you disclosed a ton of confidential information that could compromise the deal that we've been working on for months. We don't even know who has access to that fax machine; it could be anybody. I want you to create a second fax to say that "this is an example of what a deal could look like between these two companies so that whoever received the fax would view it as some type of sales pitch."

By now, everyone was looking and listening. The open floor plan gave all of us direct access to each other, and being able to shout down the hall was normal in this line of work—all in the spirit of collaboration. No one thought it was inappropriate for the banker to be yelling at me like that for what felt like ten minutes. No one came to my aid, and no one talked to me for the rest of the day. They watched and then simply went back to their grueling work as if nothing happened.

No one deserves to be yelled at like that. I tried my hardest to do a job that had little training but huge demands with very ego-driven, Ivy League-educated, privileged men. It would be a trend that I would see over and over again; the demographic pattern was consistent everywhere I went, and surprisingly, the heated exchanges among colleagues were frequent and demoralizing.

I spent the rest of that day feeling like crap. It was a career defining moment for me, and I told myself that no one should ever be treated like that, *ever*. If Brent had come back from his meeting with that fax still sitting on my desk, I still would have gotten yelled at for not doing anything with that damn fax. I couldn't win in this line of work, especially since I was a public school liberal arts major in a highly sophisticated and lucrative business. The high-pressure work and the terrible treatment were an awful mixture. People do cruel things to each other when vast sums of money are exchanged.

Being on the receiving end of such an awful exchange would inspire me later in my career to never allow anyone to treat their own colleague like that. To this day, I still can't believe that no one stood up for me or said anything to me about the situation. I know they heard Brent's tirade, but they were all trained to be silent and take it. Maybe if one person had called Brent out then I wouldn't have felt like a loser. So, I started my job hunt all over again. I must have applied to a dozen different companies, however; nothing really caught my eye. I felt stuck.

WELCOME TO START-UP LIFE

I got my lucky break when one of the bankers I worked with wanted to start his own company.

Peter was tired of the investment banking lifestyle and had the itch to do something more suited to his entrepreneurial mind. On his last week with the bank, he pulled me aside. I thought I was in trouble when he wanted to talk to me in private. I asked myself, "What mistake did I make this time?" and steeled my nerves while walking to his coveted corner office.

I sat down in Peter's huge wall-to-wall windowed office. He asked, "Mai, do you like doing what you're doing here."

I wasn't sure if it was a trick question, so I said, "Yes, it pays well and is interesting work."

He began, "Mai, I've watched you all these months, and I like the way you can juggle multiple projects with many different bankers and have good working relationships with most of the people on the floor. I think you can do better outside the confines of this bank, though."

For the first time in a long time, I received a compliment and didn't know how to react or what to say. I sat back, felt myself breathe, and listened intently. "I'm leaving the bank,"

Peter said, "and I'm starting my own company. I want you to come and help me and be my first employee!"

He mentioned he had the experience needed in business to go out on his own. However, he wasn't sure what he needed in setting up the business, finding office space, processing payroll, and hiring individuals. He was hoping I would be willing to help him.

I jumped at the chance. Even though I did not know how to do any of the things Peter mentioned, I knew it had to be better than creating one hundred-page PowerPoint decks. Plus, I could learn along the way.

This transition from investment banking into a start-up company was my first leap into the tech world. I felt I could trust Peter to have my back. He was one of the few bankers who was talented and compassionate; I admired Peter for being one of the calmest bankers on the floor. I believed he wouldn't tolerate the terrible behavior of his peers at his own company, especially if he was starting from scratch.

On my first day, I had to figure out what my priorities were, how I was going to manage my time, and how I was going to work with Peter. It was a blur looking back, but we managed to find office space a stone's throw away from the investment bank. I learned how to find accountants to process Peter's and my paychecks. Peter found a benefits/insurance broker who could help us purchase healthcare benefits ensuring that we could attract and hire employees to help us grow the business and work with us. We went shopping for a fax machine, a printer (it was the late '90s when we still needed those things), and even some silverware, dishes, and flatware for the office. Things were coming together. *This just might work*, I thought to myself.

Then, something catastrophic happened. I chose the wrong printer. Back at the bank, this would have been a surefire start to screaming match between facilities and me. I braced myself for a tongue-lashing and went to tell Peter about my mistake. Peter didn't yell at me. We simply made the replacement and went on to the next task. It was so different from my investment banking days. It was refreshing to see that Peter had not let the tough environment of investment banking harden his otherwise kind and compassionate character.

I learned a great deal in those initial months working closely with Peter and talking every single day even when he was traveling. I had to be the liaison between the accountants and lawyers. I was Peter's assistant, the company's receptionist, the office manager, and the HR manager. This would be the start of me wearing 5–6 different hats and building a variety of tools to go in my own toolkit. I thrived on the frenetic energy. We had to switch gears and get so much done in the initial phases of the business. This is where my lifelong journey (and love) of HR started.

Once we hired a full executive team, I had to present the entire benefits package to the executive team in a public forum. It was my first public speaking opportunity after years of being behind the scenes. I had butterflies in my stomach that morning, and when my turn to present came, I accidentally gave them the wrong information. I was so nervous. I couldn't keep the facts straight even though I was the one who chose all the benefit options and details. It was not my best moment, and Peter came to the rescue and helped fill in the gaps when I choked. Here in this new, supportive, and kind place, Peter chose to build a respectful business that fostered a nurturing learning environment—even one more nurturing than he had been exposed to himself. It was at this moment, I knew I made the right choice to leave the lucrative yet stressful investment banking environment. I loved the variety of my days, and wearing multiple hats and being responsible for a myriad of deliverables. This ability to multitask would set me up well for what would become a fifteen-year start-up journey. It was a lot of heavy lifting, but I thoroughly enjoyed the variety of my role. Having to handle disparate responsibilities was what allowed me to understand my passion.

This was also the start of me building a philosophy around *how* everyone should behave at work. Calling out people with their inappropriate or unprofessional behavior became my number one priority since I had witnessed and been on the receiving end of it for so long. I started to urge people to join me in creating a workplace that made work *not* suck. We needed to do this together, and with my newfound love of all things HR, I felt this was the right profession for me.

Every day as working adults, we sacrifice our time away from our closest family and friends to go to work, and I desperately wanted to make that sacrifice worth it. I created programs that treated people very well. The learning and education stipends, the healthcare benefits, the vacation time, and the perks of being an employee of a particular company were all mine to handle, and I believe I offered something that other more traditional command and control companies couldn't—a way of treating people kindly and fostering an environment that brought out the best in each other.

Peter invested at least five hours per week to train me in whatever way he could. He taught me about investment banking along the way, even though we had both left that industry. When we had time for lunch, he talked to me about his personal life and how it almost crumbled because he was traveling all the time away from his wife and two kids. Peter was the reason I fell into HR. He made sure I understood the private and public markets in which billions of dollars traded every day and taught me about how to build relationships. These lessons would serve me well as I was about to get a crash course in working in fast-paced, high-growth tech companies. I was excited; I had a passion that was centered on people, a chance to use my skills, and a boss that had my back *and* wanted to build a healthy workplace.

I wanted to be the type of leader that created workplaces that were great and best in class. I did not know that my journey would be a lonely one that seemed to have colleagues coming in and out of my life trying to counteract my desire to build kind yet high-growth businesses. It would take me years to figure out that I could not do this work by myself. If I had chosen the right colleagues or been more explicit in my own expectations then I think my path to success would not have involved me burning out and becoming somewhat jaded about how people treat each other at work. I was about to learn the hard way.

CHAPTER 2

WHERE WAS HR?

The 2017 Susan Fowler story at Uber gave rise to a global movement that empowered people to question how certain individuals get away with acts of sexual harassment, bullying, and egregious behavior while at work.[6] We've been having these discussions about diversity and inclusion in the workplace for years with, honestly, very little progress.

With the accusations lodged against high profile men like Matt Lauer, Harvey Weinstein, Charlie Rose, and many others, I started seeing stories about how HR leaders were failing in their roles. The theme of many subsequent articles across Medium, *Harvard Business Review*, and other well-respected publications was "where the hell are the HR leaders?"

The Society for Human Resource Management (SHRM) is the biggest organization that supports and educates members of the HR industry, with 285,000 members worldwide. "Our profession's highest and best value is defining and keeping a healthy culture for employees," states Johnny C. Taylor, Jr., CEO of SHRM. In some articles about workplace harassment

---

6   Susan Fowler, "Reflecting on One Very, Very Strange Year at Uber," *Susan Fowler (blog)*, February 19, 2017.

published that year, HR leaders were repeatedly "accused of protecting their organizations, or at least the powerful individuals at their helms, at the expense of the harassed workers."[7]

During my years as an HR leader, I saw many people get away with terrible behavior at work because no one was willing to call them out on inappropriate jokes, condescending words, and use of socially awkward, inappropriate language. For years, HR leaders have tried to address these workplace behaviors only for the claims to be dismissed by their—mostly male—counterparts at the executive table. Individuals who witnessed these violations feared being the whistleblower and left the coaching to the HR leaders who were, in the end, overruled by their executive teams.

In today's workplace environments, the acts of harassment happen so quickly and are so subtle that if you don't know to look for them, they can pass you by quickly. The worst part is that individuals on the receiving end of harassment refrain from speaking out because they think they might just be "too sensitive." For women, words like *mansplaining* and *hepeating* have become a part of our daily lexicon as these behaviors, while so subtle, have become so commonplace that we've begun to label them. According to the Merriam–Webster dictionary, mansplain means "to explain something to a woman in a condescending way that assumes she has no knowledge about the topic,[8]" and hepeating, which is not yet a term in the Merriam–Webster dictionary, refers to when

---

7   Dori Meinhert, "How to Investigate Sexual Harassment Allegations," *HR Magazine*, January 8, 2018.

8   *Merriam-Webster, s.v. "mansplain (v.)," accessed March 14, 2021.*

a woman suggests an idea and it's ignored but when a man says the same thing and everyone loves it.

The fact that we have created names for these behaviors finally allows women to express their true feelings around these instances that have been normalized for too long. I watched all sorts of reckless behavior and tried to pull offenders aside to give them some coaching moments. I tried to use my influence to correct them, only to feel frustrated and helpless that my coaching wasn't working. I coached a new college graduate who didn't know how to make the transition from frat house life to work life; I coached someone who told me he tried to limit himself to seventeen—*seventeen!*—drinks per work event and even tried to stop one of our leaders from using "f*ck" in every sentence. It seemed that they couldn't or wouldn't change especially because they worked in an informal, casual environment. Examples like these are what foster a very fraternity-like culture (a.k.a. bro culture) that women, minorities, and any diverse populations have to stomach.

Since I am an HR leader, and because I see these behaviors in the workplace, I always make sure to be the HR person in the room anytime we have annual reviews, compensation decisions, or promotion discussions as a leadership group. As much as I tried to standardize the criteria for all these matters, I once witnessed the quiet but effective Hispanic customer service agent receive the most doubt when it came to compensation increases or promotions.

"Has anyone told the guy that he has dandruff?" These were the words that caused the engineer's chances for leadership to be doomed. The question "If he is so quiet, can he really lead?" spelled disaster for any type of upward mobility for the hardworking engineer from Southeast Asia. They did nothing wrong, they just didn't fit nicely into the mold of the typical corporate America ladder climber—confident, charismatic, and extroverted.

"Mai, you need to tell Michael that he has dandruff and he should really wash his hair more often or get it treated. It's also your job to get Max in front of us so that we can get to know him more and really assess his future with the company. We don't know anything about him because he's so quiet. Oh, and while you're talking to Michael and Max, can you also tell Brittany and Sarah that they need to settle their differences and move on? They are still bickering about the commission on one particular client, and it's distracting the entire sales team."

I thought I had failed as an HR leader since I didn't even think to approach Michael about his dandruff; I never even thought to schedule time to talk to Max about him being too quiet or address the Brittany–Sarah dynamic. I knew these were all issues for them, but I did not realize I had so much authority to sidestep their own managers. I also knew that none of these people reported to me, so why would they listen to me? Managers need to have these direct conversations with their own reports—not rely on HR to do the dirty work.

I told the leader that mentioned Michael's dandruff that he needed to have that conversation himself, not me. He asked, "What am I supposed to tell him? That's going to be so awkward. Why can't you handle that conversation, Mai? You'd be so much more diplomatic than me."

I responded, "You're the one that sees the problem. As a leader, I expect you to deal with it since he's on your team, not mine. I need your help since I can't be the only leader that has these types of conversations. We're all in this together, and

I can't be the one that gives difficult feedback to employees. Besides, he's not even in my own department."

It was then that I decided to write a book. I was tired of people pointing their fingers at HR leaders—the people who, for years (maybe even decades), were sworn to silence as they tried to discreetly handle these "delicate" problems. I'm not sure having dandruff should make or break someone's career progression.

As much as I tried to build work environments where people could thrive, I felt that I was alone in wanting adults to act their age at work. Michael's boss couldn't have a conversation about his hygiene habits, so Michael never made it to a leadership position and probably never knew why. Max's manager couldn't give him more exposure to other people, so Max ended up being a career manager even though his dream was to become a vice president. It was sad for me to witness these situations, but I didn't and couldn't spend my time doing everyone else's job.

I hosted manager trainings every Thursday for a span of six months where I attempted to teach managers everything I knew—how to motivate individuals, how to drive effective one-on-one meetings, how to become a leader. None of these trainings sunk in for the people that needed them the most. We bought copies and studied books like Kim Scott's *Radical Candor*, but none of those books or trainings seemed to work either. I scratched my head constantly trying to understand what was wrong.

Employees working in the world of tech pay homage to those leaders who are serial entrepreneurs and who made millions of dollars at a young age. These leaders have risen quickly, are sometimes the smartest people in the room, and have no fear of disrupting whatever industry they work in. Leadership teams in Silicon Valley are filled with these recurrent and successful entrepreneurs. They get away with questionable behavior because their sole focus is to build private companies that offer an exit strategy and a fast way to make millions of dollars. They choose not to focus too much on training and investing in their leaders and instead focus on the promise of a quick buck.

Building a product that the world didn't know it needed and capturing sales for that same product can yield millions of dollars in an initial public offering (IPO), merger and acquisition (M&A), or any other type of exit transaction. As part of a standard compensation package at a start-up, employees get equity in the form of stock options. These stock options give you the option to buy shares in a company once it has a "liquid event." This event creates a path that allows many employees to make millions. The stock options are sometimes granted at a strike price of pennies on the dollar so that when a company has an exit transaction, that same option can be worth more than twenty dollars on the open market. It's called paper money in the beginning and can turn into a golden ticket for many people who join a start-up well before the liquid event happens.

Many first-time CEOs blaze their own paths to success, and even though they say they care about culture, some of the ones I've worked with create very bro-ish cultures. These cultures may include a focus on sports, games, money, and generally very male-dominated topics of conversation. They don't pay attention to how those things create a culture that makes individuals not interested in these subjects feel excluded or, worse, rejected.

These same CEOs can make one transaction worth millions of dollars, so many people want to work alongside the next Mark Zuckerberg (CEO of Facebook) or Travis Kalanick (former CEO of Uber). All the inappropriate behavior gets dismissed especially when employees stand to make millions by being in these tech start-ups at the right moment. The money from an IPO, an M&A, or any other equity transaction can change your life. I've seen multiple employees follow CEOs moving from start-up to start-up because they are making money each time they hitch a ride, even when they don't respect the CEO.

In a *Forbes* article from 2013, five-time CEO Michael Wolfe spells out three ways to get rich working in a start-up technology company:

1. Join a successful company when they have less than one hundred employees;
2. Join a moderately successful company as an executive; and
3. Build your own company.[9]

Although the timeline for working in a start-up and having a potential transaction has lengthened, I find that many young employees can make substantial amounts of money working in a start-up. Millions of dollars for twenty- or thirty-something-year-old employees is life changing; equity, especially in the form of stock options, can be worth six figures or seven figures in one single transaction. I still remember attending three different retirement parties for our friends who made so much money that they never needed to work another day in their lives—all before they turned thirty-five years old.

---

9   Micheal Wolfe, "The Three Ways to Make a Lot of Money at a Startup," *Forbes, October 31, 2013*.

Beverly, a finance and HR (dual hatted) leader, thinks about what that much money does to people. She came from the world of nonprofits and chose to spend her last ten years as a serial tech leader instead. "There is a lot of good in tech, and there's a lot of good people. I think, ultimately, what really ended up souring the whole thing is that it was all about making a quick buck, and I think that's not a great way to be in the world. I don't think tech is solving very many problems at all."

HR leaders are constantly in the background trying to make these workplaces healthy; however, the leader, or CEO, of the organization is often the one that sets the tone for the culture. They typically lay the foundation for the culture based on how they behave at work. What they do and what they say gives employees a clear stance on what is acceptable behavior. Larry Kim, the CEO of MobileMonkey, encourages all CEOs to "be very intentional to project the values you wish to be adopted at your start-up company."[10]

HR leaders, and other managers, know who the problematic individuals are in their companies. If a CEO or leadership team doesn't have time to address HR issues, then the behaviors linger. In some ways, the fast growth and real potential to make money and disrupt traditional industries overshadow any principles around morality or professionalism.

The focus on what they call "f*ck you money" overshadowed any version of creating a great workplace.

The inability for leaders to coach their own teams and their reliance on me to have difficult conversations to address any type of inappropriate behavior reflect the rollercoaster

---

10   Larry Kim, "Building a Great Startup Culture Starts with the Founder," Medium, December 20, 2016.

of my professional life. Some days I felt good about the progress I was making toward eliminating bias and inappropriate behaviors, while other days I knew that I was running in place.

I was always in the room trying to do my job, but in a battle of CEO versus HR leader, HR always loses.

CHAPTER 3

THE CEO CHAPTER

—

Most tech CEOs are visionary leaders who like to disrupt the world through change. I've worked with six different start-up CEOs. Most of them were serial entrepreneurs who built companies, sold them, and then went on to create more businesses. While I always admired their brilliant business minds, I also got the chance to see all of their flaws. My conclusion is that the "C" in CEO stands for **crazy**.

With me, they let down their professional guards and showed me their true personality traits. I've seen them lie in front of their board of directors; I knew who evaded taxes for years; I've been the therapist to their own personal dating disasters. Conversely, I also knew the other dimensions of their character; they were charming when they needed to be, and some of them were so devoted to their families that they would not schedule any meetings past 5:00 p.m. in order for everyone to make it home at a decent time. I knew one CEO who would conduct his own exit interviews with departing employees as a way of apologizing for things not working out. They all had their own unique leadership styles. Only some of them truly believe that employees are their company's greatest asset.

One of my favorite traits, though, is that they can adapt to any environment.

Switching personas isn't easy for anyone, but these tech start-up CEOs whom I've worked with can context switch as fast as Gal Gadot can transform into Wonder Woman. Jam-packed days don't allow for a lot of downtime, so I've seen them jump on planes at the last minute, take calls with investors, answer to the board, and have an all-hands meeting at a moment's notice, all without breaking a sweat.

That sounds like a full day, right? I'd gotten so used to seeing them switch gears and adapt to the people in the room with such ease that I took it for granted how hard they worked. They used a different altitude of communication to convey information to the board, who they technically report to, and deliver a more generous flow of information to the rest of the company. It was like magic to watch them shift gears and shift focus. I loved that part of my job.

For two years, I worked with Robert, the CEO of a global start-up. He was a visionary and a serial entrepreneur. He had some previous successes with his other start-ups, so he carried himself with an air of gravitas and arrogance. Deep inside, he was a jerk.

I remember Robert urged me to launch what we called a global mobility program. Since we had offices all over the world, the program would allow employees in each office to travel to different offices to live and work for weeks at a time. While this program would have been a perk to most people, I found it hard to execute. I had to think about taxes, time zones for calls, and schools for those with children. It's hard to uproot families for a tour of duty into a foreign country, especially if you're not set up to offer support for the adjustment. Instead of hearing about the complications I had to solve, Robert looked at me with some annoyance and said, "just figure it out," dismissing all of the complex logistics that were involved. He said, "I thought you were smarter than that," as he walked away.

I was hurt. He treated my work flippantly and made me feel dumb for making a big deal out of operational matters, for which he cared little. He might as well of given me a piece of red tape.

I worked closely with this man for two years. I knew he was disappointed in me. I was standing in the way of developing a program that would have been distinctive to a company of our size. I desperately wanted to deliver on it. I worked tirelessly, needing to work with tax attorneys, employment lawyers, and different HR and benefits vendors. It was a ton of heavy lifting to get this thing off the ground.

The next day, Robert waltzed into my office and apologized for making me feel like sh*t. He knew I was explaining the barriers to the program. He acknowledged that certain programs needed more support than we could offer. He offered to take me to lunch. We spent that lunch hour talking about our personal lives, making me feel like we were best friends reuniting; he made that switch from jerk to buddy so quickly I forgot about the scars from the conversation which only happened the day before.

I began to spot a pattern: Robert took pride in humiliating me in front of people. He challenged my knowledge as a way of making me perform out of my comfort zone. I still recall a second episode when Robert chided me for a chart I had displayed at an executive meeting. He chuckled and then said, "Mai, you can't put these graphs on top of each other. It looks like you are fudging the numbers." I'm sure I turned red, embarrassed, and doubting my own work.

Luckily my colleagues came to my defense to let Robert know that these numbers weren't fudged and the graphs showed exactly what was intended, which was that our employee engagement scores were plummeting.

Robert didn't acknowledge their thoughts in the meeting and said, "I need Mai to give us better visualizations that represent a true picture. I still don't believe these are the right facts or numbers." He moved the agenda forward not allowing anyone to challenge his thinking. We all sat in silence letting him drone on for the next hour.

Afterward, I sat down with Robert to show him the numbers and articulate why I placed the graphs the way I did. He agreed with me that it was the right way to show the numbers, and now that he had seen the numbers, he could not doubt them.

Again, he apologized, "Sorry, Mai, I did not mean to embarrass you like that in front of the executive team." I forgave him and moved on. That Friday, I received a lovely bouquet of flowers from him with a note that read, "Sorry I embarrassed you in front of others. I really do believe in you!"

The apology

I can recall countless episodes of this pattern—everything going well, then an abusive slap or knock on my work followed by an apology. I had to recover from the abuse, accept the nice presents of time with him—lunches and flowers—and then get back up to wait for the next slap. If I wanted to keep my job, then I had to endure the humiliation.

Kristen, who is a five-time HR leader, shared some of her own CEO stories that have a similar theme: "Jeff literally shut me down in meetings. If I said anything not related to HR, he would interrupt me to say, 'I actually don't care what you have to say about the business, you don't understand the business. I've heard enough from you.'" She learned to grow immune to the many insults she had to endure. She stayed in the HR field for years knowing that she knew how to build successful companies despite working with some very young and inexperienced CEOs.

Kristen also recounted the story about one of the other CEOs she worked with who walked around the building at 8:00 every night with a clipboard taking notes of who was in their seat working and who had left for the evening. She was frequently asked to sit in meetings between the CEO and his executive direct reports where he would yell and throw things at his direct reports for multiple hours. More than once, Kristen had to respectfully stop the conversation and, after allowing him to cool off, coach him on better ways to express his frustration with the team.

When she started at another start-up, Billy would cut her off at meetings and not allow her to finish her own sentences. He would "forget" to copy Kristen on executive team emails, and then he would blindside her by asking an executive peer to "coach" her. He would then proceed to chastise her in meetings in front of her peers. He frequently called last-minute meetings on Sundays that lasted for hours requiring the leadership team to listen to his rants. If anybody was busy and not available, he made it clear that was unacceptable.

Kristen explained, "I thought I was the crazy one since he always made me feel like I wasn't doing enough for his company. Looking back, I have too many examples where I can see clearly that he is the crazy one—not me."

What I've learned from working with many CEOs is that I rarely win an argument with the leader of the company, even when I'm presenting the right thing to do. If the business isn't doing well, they want to administer layoffs quickly and swiftly. Start-up CEOs don't have historical data to help them make informed decisions, but one of their biggest fears is running out of cash or having to raise another round of funding without being able to control their destiny. On the contrary, if the business is performing ahead of the financial forecast, they want to accelerate full steam ahead and hire more people to sustain the revenue lift to move faster.

Working alongside these powerful CEOs, I've hired thousands of people in short spans of time, and I've also executed layoffs in about a third of the companies where I've worked. It's a vicious cycle to go from the highs of booming sales to the lows of flat revenue, even after multiple iterations.

Living through the adrenaline rush from the highs and lows of working with these talented CEOs, I realized that I'm married to this individual while at work. I have to live with them every day through the abuse and joys of choosing to be in that relationship. I spent many hours trying to build this relationship because I needed this person to trust me. I used my influence to drive an HR strategy that was connected to the business. If the CEO empowered me to own the HR function and trusted me, I knew I could execute a vision that treated employees well. If I reacted too quickly, I would lose credibility because they would think I was trying to judge them. I learned how to flex my leadership style to any audience so that I became a chameleon just like them. Over time, I learned to hold my tongue to fight only certain battles, which ended up being the key to my own sanity.

I discovered that this unchecked conduct happens at many different start-ups. Speaking with Odette, an HR leader who has worked at two start-ups, I found her own experience similar to my own: "The personal beliefs of the CEO trickle down like dominoes; there is always a mirroring that happens. If the CEO says or does something, it's okay for everyone else to say or do that same thing or behave in that same way. That might work when a company is really small, but as it grows and scales, those episodes become part of a bigger pool. I think if leaders don't care about these indiscretions enough to either change or stop them, then these moments go unchecked. These instances and behaviors define the real culture of the start-up."

Looking back, I realize that my CEO was the one I should have focused on the most to create lasting change. The CEO, as well as the rest of the executive team, sets the tone for how the rest of the company behaves. Tone starts from the top, and I did not realize I was focused on coaching managers when I should have been focused on the executive team. I assumed the executive team didn't need my help.

That assumption would dig me further into the abyss of running in place, *alone*. I switched jobs often, especially after I grew weary of not moving the needle fast enough on issues of diversity and inclusion feeling constantly disappointed at the bro-ish environments I tended to be attracted to.

Little did I know that the work of calling inappropriate behaviors out in the workplace would lead more rocks to topple down on me. I felt flattened like a pancake on most days, and I knew that others sat by and watched: Some leaders even sat back and enjoyed the organic popcorn we offered as part of our snack selection while watching me drown in the drama.

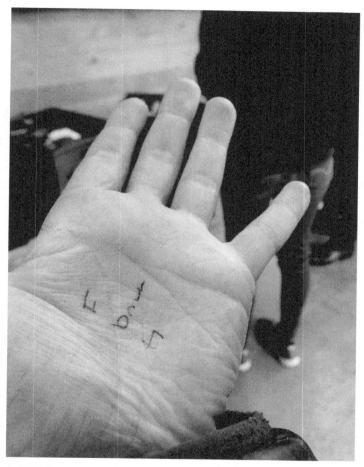

A CEO keeping track of what he wanted to discuss with me while on our afternoon walk/meeting.

CHAPTER 4

ON BEING (NOT) BLACK

Slack is an instant messenger tool that is used to communicate quick bursts of information. One of my CEOs adopted it as his favorite mode of communication. He posted photos, jokes, and sent funny one-liners frequently. I laughed most of the time, until one day when he posted something very unbecoming of a CEO.

We had one month to launch a marketing campaign that was supposed to generate millions of dollars in new revenue. The team worked at least seventy hours in the last week to prepare and complete the project. As you can imagine, a lot of marketing work requires the efforts of product, public relations, and creative teams together. Someone on the marketing team snapped a photo of the team and called it "Apple iPhoto stock–worthy." The photo captured an entire twenty-person team, working in a twelve-by-twelve conference room and laughing even though they all looked tired. The photo landed on a Slack channel for the entire company to see.

It wasn't long before my CEO added a comment to the photo: "It's not Apple iPhoto–worthy because we are missing a Black person."

As I read his post, my heart sank. He was trying to be funny although I don't think many would find it funny. I didn't know whether to laugh or cry; I was dizzy with emotion and couldn't put my finger on what made his post inappropriate. On the one hand, he finally saw that we lacked diversity in the company, and on the other hand, why did he have to point it out in such a flippant way?

I felt the need to find out.

I got up from desk, used my hands to iron out the wrinkles from my dress, and marched down the sunlit hallway to his corner office. Without saying hello, I barged into his office.

"What were you thinking?" I growled in a hushed tone.

Clearly, he knew what I was talking about. "When Apple takes a stock photo, they usually represent a diverse group," he said simply. "Women, men, Black, White, Hispanic, Asian, young, old…all types of people are included. We're missing a Black person."

He leaned back in his chair and smiled, pleased with his response. I relaxed my shoulders a little; I'm not sure why exactly. I knew talking to him would make me understand his intentions better.

"Not everyone knows your sense of humor, Andy. What else do you notice about the photo? Did you realize the funniest thing about the photo is that everyone looks like sh*t in the photo? Or what about simply saying, 'Thank you for busting your butt to get this campaign out the door?'"

He wasn't budging and looked at me like I was crazy.

He stared at me and asked, "Mai, I take it you didn't find that funny?"

"Not really, Andy, no. I wish you would have said something like 'we need to hire more people from different backgrounds and identities so we can build a more diverse community here' or something to that effect. Instead, you chose to shoot straight from the hip and make a flippant comment. I don't want that comment to get misconstrued. Imagine if someone grabbed a screenshot of that and posted it to social media? I think you'd be embarrassed, right?"

I could tell he was tiring of the conversation, and with a deadpan expression, he said, "Nope."

I left his office wanting to stick my middle finger up in the air at him; I did it in my mind.

When I returned to my desk, I looked at the Slack message and realized that twenty-six people had liked it and ten people had reacted with the laughing face emoji. Was I the only one who was seeing a problem with this remark or, worse, making a big deal out of nothing again? How can everyone just go back to business as usual?

I tried to help Andy see that he was more than just Andy; he was the CEO of our company, and his behaviors had a trickle-down effect throughout the rest of the company. In these small moments, he sends signals and clues to employees of what he thinks is acceptable. He sets the culture and tone for everyone else.

The line is super thin in tech start-ups. Most of the CEOs I worked with gave everyone the benefit of the doubt and assumed good intentions. The problem is if the CEO allows certain conduct to go unchecked then it allows employees to act in the same way, and before you know it, you've created a toxic culture. It is a slippery slope that is hard to reverse; a racist joke here and there can be dismissed if someone of that race tells it. Just because you are of a certain race does *not* make it okay for you to tell a racist joke. That's not how it works.

I knew I was in a unique position to help shape what I viewed as ways to be lighthearted at work but still uphold professional practices. I became the only one that questioned leaders and their unprofessional behavior. I learned how to have difficult conversations to shed some light on how tone-deaf leaders were to their own words. I grew confident in having these discussions because I saw too many episodes of people getting away with inappropriate behavior. I had nothing to lose and everything to gain if I wanted to create a workplace that was more inclusive, so I forced myself to speak up, always thinking about Emma and the future generations in the background.

In some companies, I made headway with leaders who seriously had no clue about the weight of their words and actions. None of them were malicious; all of them lacked self-awareness and needed some coaching to recognize their own patterns. I could see that some CEOs were trying to be more careful with their tone and words based on the audience they had in front of them. I even created a gesture for one particular CEO who needed coaching in the moment: When I tugged on my left ear that was our secret sign for him to try to rephrase the sentence he just uttered. Those were wonderful moments when I could see the impact of my high effort. In other companies, I felt gaslit constantly for trying to correct these behaviors; leaders sometimes ignored me, laughed at me, or even made me feel that I was making a big deal out of nothing. Was I the crazy one?

Increasing the inclusion of underrepresented populations—particularly the Black, Latinx, Indigenous American, and Asian Pacific Islander communities—is a real struggle in tech start-ups. Beverly, who we met in chapter 2, told me about a Black woman who she hired at her company as an office manager. Over the years, this woman was encouraged by the engineering team and taught herself how to code so that she could become an engineer. Once she joined the engineering team, they grew to be one of the most diverse departments in the company. We all need role models, and we've all seen that it just takes one person to unlock the power of seeing and believing.

Even in those companies where I couldn't break through, I never gave up the fight to build great workplaces where we treated each other with more empathy and with more inclusive etiquette. I was determined to show Emma's generation that they wouldn't have to live through the same episodes we did.

CHAPTER 5

MEDITATION & PING-PONG TABLES

———

Sheila liked to meditate. She had spent twenty years practicing the ancient art, taking a ten-minute break at exactly 3:00 p.m. every day to recenter herself. It didn't matter how busy she was. Sheila always found time for self-care. I admired her for the commitment she had to the practice. It was easy to watch Sheila meditate. Each time I walked by her in that southeast corner of the office, I felt at peace.

Sheila was our in-house recruiter. In the fast-paced world of tech start-ups, we sometimes set goals to hit 100 percent headcount growth year over year. We operated at breakneck speed trying to find talent. Our managers spent twenty hours a week on interviews, barely keeping pace with their day jobs. Sheila was the dedicated recruiter to John. John was not a fan of Sheila nor Sheila's meditation practice, especially not during work hours.

In the first quarter, John had a revenue goal that was the biggest one in the company's history. The pressure of hiring and building a sales team that could drive that much revenue was keeping him up at night.

He walked over to my desk one morning and asked to talk to me.

"It'll only take five minutes," he promised as he slumped down at my desk. I sighed. Any time someone tells you that something will only take five minutes, just know it won't.

"I have a problem with Sheila taking a meditation break every day," he said. "My team is under a ton of pressure to produce sales, and it actually stresses us out to see Sheila sitting there and doing nothing. She does it every day at 3:00 p.m. in our corner of the office, and it's annoying as f*ck."

I had to collect myself before responding. *What's the big deal?* I thought to myself. And who exactly was "us"? Was his entire sales team, which was predominantly male, bothered by her daily ritual?

Studies were beginning to show what we always knew: Breaks lead to less burnout and more focused thinking. Hell, Cal Newport wrote the book *Deep Work* which even encouraged people to practice being bored.[11] I really couldn't see what the problem was. Everyone took all sorts of breaks—smoking, walking, and praying to name a few. I knew John's team took ping-pong breaks throughout the day. Why should Sheila's meditation be a problem to them?

I looked at John and asked if members of his team take a break to play ping-pong every day. He answered, "Yes, but what does that have to do with Sheila?"

I took a deep breath and faced him. "What's the big deal, John? Members of your team play ping-pong Every Day.

---

11   Cal Newport, *Deep Work: Rules for Focused Success in a Distracted World* (New York: Grand Central Publishing, 2016).

Sometimes, they play more than once a day. Why are they all up in arms about Sheila taking a meditation break?"

I asked another question without allowing him to answer my first question: "Why doesn't it bother you when your own team members, who have to sell and deliver these huge sales targets, take breaks?

He replied, "It's what they do to de-stress; they need to whack that ball, sometimes, Mai."

I could tell he was getting impatient with me.

"What's the difference between the ping-pong table and meditation?" I asked.

He lost his temper and yelled at me, "I just wanted to let you know that I'm bothered by Sheila's meditation! Can you just tell her to practice it somewhere else because I don't want to be around to see it?" He cleared his throat. "My point is that I don't think it's acceptable for her to take a break like that when I know that she has a lot of hiring to do and my team has a lot of sales to deliver."

In a calm tone, I tried my best to explain to him: "Each of us has different ways of de-stressing. Some people like to smash a small, white plastic ball while others like to sit in silence. I'm not going to squash Sheila's daily meditation ritual just as I won't squash anyone's table tennis games."

He looked at me incredulously, and he literally asked if he could kindly have the conversation with Sheila himself. I told him I wouldn't stop him from doing such a thing, but would he mind if I had the same conversation with his own sales team about playing ping-pong? I could tell he didn't like my answer. He walked away with nothing left to add. Sheila kept her meditation habit, and the sales guys kept their table tennis games.

Looking back at this conversation, I realize that this silly office squabble was about more than Sheila and her meditation habits. This was about how my companies and coworkers viewed women in the workplace. Certain things like ping-pong tables are acceptable forms of life at tech companies. For John and his sales team, meditation was not an acceptable form of play (or rest). I think the femininity of something like meditation—relaxed, restful, calm, soothing—was in stark contrast to the aggression of tabletop games like ping-pong, foosball, or billiards where you could literally crush your opponent.

If you walk through any tech start-up office space, you're likely to find either a ping-pong table, a foosball table, or a billiards table. As a matter of fact, most of the bigger technology companies have all three and more.[12]

Generally speaking, those types of games are accepted toys for most tech companies. In fact, it was typically one of the first pieces of furniture I ordered every time we opened a new office; it was almost never an option to *not* get at least one of those toys. In my eyes, these types of games, although meant for a little playfulness at work, turned into one of the symbols of a male-dominated culture. I never built any yoga or meditation rooms at these same companies.

In all the companies where I worked, these game tables were a requisite part of start-up culture. The office tours we hosted for potential candidates carved a path into the game room to proudly promote and show that we were cool and "had it made." Some companies even had bar-like pubs built into their office space; it was part of the drinking culture that

---

12 Aamna Mohdin, "If Ping-Pong Table Sales Are Falling, Then Silicon Valley Is Clearly Doomed," *Quartz, May 4, 2016.*

dominated so much of start-up life. Being able to showcase the fancy Tornado Classic foosball table, the $89 Killerspin ping-pong paddles, or the customized billiards table was usually the highlight of any office tour.

We had all the fun toys and symbols to represent that we were successful, but the outside sparkle was merely a facade. Inside, we were running in place with so much to build and do. It was pure chaos, and on certain days we felt we would suffer death by a thousand cuts because of all the small decisions we made with no time or history on which to base our decisions. There was so much focus on "fun," even when the business wasn't quite steady.

Working in start-ups is actually hard work. The fun environments can look alluring, but scratch beneath the surface and you will find the sparkly veneer is even less than dull. The work-life balance, games, and great work environments must be weighed with your own tolerance for operating in the gray area where the infrastructure for the company isn't built yet. You are putting the pieces together into a jigsaw puzzle that has no template. Some people sacrifice their peace of mind and tolerate the chaos for the ability to launch their careers quickly.

In the end, tech start-ups are not for everyone. You must decide if you can thrive without guidelines or frameworks for how you do your work. People over-rotate when choosing a fun work environment and find out quickly that they have to work with ambiguity. If you like solving a series of moving puzzle pieces without a template, then consider joining a start-up. If you don't, then run far and fast in a different direction.

CHAPTER 6

THE CALM BEFORE
THE STORM

———

Views of the San Francisco Bay never get old. I once worked for a company that had sweeping views of the Bay Bridge. Every day I would walk into work looking out at the blue skies before I started my day. Mondays were our executive team meetings. Similar to almost every company, Mondays were a little hectic. One sunny day, we were preparing for our quarterly board meeting trying to solve the issue of one particular board member who would always fall asleep in our meetings. We couldn't figure out if he was bored, tired, or just uninterested, so we spent this morning talking about how we could keep him awake.

We spent long hours working. Thank goodness we had fabulous views of the San Francisco Bay.

Seated around the long, oval-shaped marble table, we were fully focused. When we got to slide forty-two, our VP of customer success (CS) made a really inappropriate joke. I don't remember the joke, but I will never forget my reaction to it.

I lost my composure. "You know, I don't think it's appropriate to make these kinds of jokes. I can't believe you all feel that this is okay. I'm actually tired of being the only one that calls people out. We're all adults in this room. We're all the leaders of this company, and I can't believe that you're letting the VP of CS get away with jokes like this."

What happened afterward was the CEO looked at me and said, "calm down" using his palms to signal me to take it down a notch.

I lost it again, and I said, "You know what? F*ck you! How is this appropriate that you're letting our VP of CS get away with this stuff? I'm passionate about this stuff because I'm the only woman at the table, and it sucks. It's lonely, I feel isolated, and you guys don't seem to recognize that it makes it really hard for me to sit here with you on certain days for hours at a time enduring these jokes."

He said, "Mai we have so many things to cover in the agenda. So, I understand, you didn't find Steven's joke funny, but let's move on." And that's how it was left; my whole statement about having to endure these inappropriate behaviors landed flat.

Afterward the CEO sent me a Slack message that said, "I had no idea you were so passionate about diversity. Honestly, I didn't think about you being the only woman. You're accepted into this executive team so I didn't think about it, but I care about these issues as much as you do. I want to help do something about it, so let's start."

He suggested some ideas around how we could make our workplace better, one of them being a secret shopper program where a secret person comes into the interview process to figure out if we have bias in our interview process. A few other ideas included more trainings around bias and even donations to fund causes outside of the normal Silicon Valley picks.

Although we did not bring in secret shoppers (it was too much effort), we devoted more budget to hiring external trainers on diversity in the workplace. We increased the dialogue around sensitive moments, and we made a dedicated effort to be more inclusive. We displayed more thoughtful touches like ordering a variety of food for our in-office lunch meetings. We finally understood that many people have allergies to different things, so ordering sandwiches all these years meant we were neglecting vegans/vegetarians, gluten-free needs, and employees who typically don't eat sliced meats. We no longer ordered unisex T-shirts or hoodies either; we again realized that by making clothing unisex, the clothing was made for no one. Gender-specific batches of clothing provided a more thoughtful way for everyone to feel that we customized them for each individual. This underwater effort to make our company more inclusive was actually uplifting because I believed we were finally doing the right thing. Those moments made me smile even though I knew I had to tackle bigger, more systemic issues with our leadership team.

Still, I didn't feel that the CEO accepted me for who I was, AND I felt strange knowing that he didn't recognize that I was the only woman at his table.

I saved that Slack message so that I could reflect on it years later. I realize now that most CEOs were actually on my side. The choice came down to whether they wanted to spend time on correcting their own or their leaders' behaviors or focusing their time and energy on the business. Most of the CEOs I worked with chose the business over training their leaders.

Over the years, I felt so lonely. I was tired of being the only adult at the table. The workplace and the jokes seemed to be all the same—inappropriate. The only thing that changed was the physical location through the years. I wish I had more advocates in the room. As an HR leader, it was my duty to give people feedback so that they could grow professionally, although often this type of criticism made me feel like a mother. Some of my peers called me a motherf*cker. I was exhausted from fighting this fight. I'm not sure how many times that rock rolled back onto me.

I had more fight to give.

CHAPTER 7

BURPING, FARTING, AND OTHER NOISES

———

It was springtime in San Francisco; the morning air was crisp, almost refreshing. I watched from our conference room window as the sun broke through the heavy fog. It was going to be a beautiful day.

Light poured into the room, brightening our dark space. My executive team sat around the conference room table, coffee cups perched by their sides. It was a 9:00 morning meeting that was supposed to last for two and a half hours. Tangled computer cords were draped everywhere over the marble conference room table. *So much for using that functional center panel*, I thought to myself. We installed fancy furniture and hidden panels to tuck computer cables underneath the table and hide all the cables, though we never seemed to tuck them under. The fancy designs were merely a showpiece. Why ask me to pick out some sophisticated design elements for our office space if they were okay with messy cables that made our space look like a college dorm room? I shook my head. Men...

My CEO cleared his throat and launched into the day's agenda, careful not to waste any time. We sat around the table for the better part of three hours, going slide by slide through a beautiful but painfully boring slideshow. Twenty-five slides down, fifteen to go—it was like we were in our own personal hell. Suddenly Rob, one of the men to my right, popped out of his chair.

"Biobreak!" Rob yelled as he bolted out of the room.

A collective sigh of relief washed over the room. We were all thinking how bored we were staring at a slideshow. This was not the best use of our time on a Monday morning.

As another coworker, Mark, shifted in his seat, he laughed and said to Rob, "Wimp, can't you hold your pee?"

Rob stopped dead in his tracks and never made it out the door before Mark started to tell a story.

Mark's father is a gastroenterologist (a GI doctor). When Mark was young, his father claimed that a man's bladder can expand to the size of a basketball: "The sign of a strong man is determined by how long he can hold his pee. The longer he can hold his pee, the stronger he is." Occasionally Mark's father tested his "strength" by seeing how long he could go without using the restroom. If he could not last through noon, his father called him a wimp.

Mark was now calling Rob a wimp. Rob turned to Mark and responded, "F*ck that, I'm going to the bathroom."

It was a funny interaction, and I had a front row seat to what I consider to be a male pissing contest. No pun intended. I rolled my eyes at the immaturity of this moment. I wonder what would have happened if I needed a break to use the bathroom. Would Mark have told me the same story?

I sat through stories and events that became common (and comical) for me. Working in a male-dominated field, you have to develop a thick skin in order to survive. Over the course of my fifteen years in tech, I became impervious to the many noises, jokes, and smells that would waft down the halls, and these moments still stick with me. I grew tolerant of all sorts of episodes so that I could survive.

Open office floorplans dominate the tech start-up scene

Speaking of noises, bathrooms in the office spaces of male-dominated tech companies are probably the one area that works in favor of women. Working in tech start-ups usually means you'll be working in an open office floor plan. These spaces were quite the rage in tech start-ups back in the early 2000s and even in present day. They offered flexible working stations and high levels of collaboration, and, honestly, you can fit more people into an open floor plan.[13]

---

13   Katharine Schwab, "Everyone Hates Open Offices. Here's Why They Still Exist," *Fast Company, January 15, 2019.*

While the workspaces these open floor plans provide us are collaborative and cool, almost every office I worked in ran into the same problem: the restrooms in each of these commercial office spaces were never meant to accommodate the one hundred plus people we crammed into one floor. Since most of the companies where I worked were at least 80 percent men, it was the first time that men were waiting in line to use the bathroom.

Men complained about waiting in line or dubbed it unfair that we didn't have enough restrooms for them, even though it's an inconvenience most women experience on a regular basis. This was the first time that I finally found the benefit of working with so many men: They could finally understand what it felt like to feel deprived of a need so reasonable.

Some of the men couldn't wait, so they occasionally snuck into the women's restroom "to take a leak," as they so crudely put it. They didn't realize the women knew exactly when they were doing it. Some men played coy as they were caught leaving our bathrooms making up some lame excuse when caught: "I heard a leaking sound, so I went into the women's restroom to check on it." *Right.*

What the men never knew was that the women in the office honestly never minded if they used the ladies room. We all knew how it felt to wait in line to use a bathroom, and, hell, I'm sure a couple of us even popped into a men's room when the line for the ladies' room was too long in the other venues of our life. Still, the men felt the need to come up with these lame excuses to try and save face in the office.

When I clocked five full days of men sneaking into the ladies' restrooms, I penned an email to the office because both restrooms were beginning to look like unattended train station bathrooms—filled with newspapers, toilet paper, and even water on the floors (at least I hope it was water). It was disgusting. Once I clicked send on the email, my inbox got slammed with responses like, "Who's leaving boogers on the walls? Please clean up after the sh*t coming out of your nose." It still makes me cringe that men would reply and openly write even more revolting stories.

Beverly, the HR leader who hired the office manager turned engineer, confirms my sneaking suspicion: "Men, mostly White men, are all so individually genuine and thoughtful and caring. You put them at the table together, and they make it a good ole boys' club." They use language such as "penetrating the market" and "we're now pregnant with this client and have to see it through," expressions which are irritating at best.

Burping, farting, and many other noises permeated the hallways of the tech companies where I worked. It was sickening to any professional adult. The combination of a lax environment and a slightly immature workforce made these episodes acceptable. All these stories still make me wince; they were my reality for so long that I stopped flinching. As a woman, I normalized all these moments as a defense mechanism and a survival tactic. My skin got thicker through the years.

In some ways, working in a start-up can feel like being in college, where you have access to plenty of activities, have freedom to manage your own schedule, and hang out with your colleagues, who you believe to be your friends, all day long.

Just when I thought I'd experienced everything that was divisive about start-up life, I would soon find out that it was only the tip of the iceberg.

CHAPTER 8

ON BEING A
WOMAN IN TECH

———

In most of the companies where I worked, women made up only 20 to 30 percent of the workforce and, worse, made up less than 10 percent of the executive teams. What's even more dramatic is that women, and every gender category outside of men, would score 10–20 percentage points lower on the quarterly employee engagement surveys.

Culture Amp, a survey platform designed to measure employee engagement, has administered over 31,000 surveys and defines employee engagement as the levels of enthusiasm and connection employees have with their organization. It's a measure of how motivated people are to put in extra effort for their organization and a sign of how committed they are to staying there.[14]

Value statements are used to determine an employee engagement score. On a scale of one to five, where one is

---

14   Alexis Croswell, "What Is Employee Engagement?" *Culture Amp (blog),* *accessed February 24, 2021.*

low and five is high, employees rate their companies on statements such as the following:

1. I would recommend our company as a great place to work.
2. I rarely think about looking for work outside of this company.
3. I see myself still working here in two years.
4. I am proud to work for this company.
5. I am motivated to go beyond what I would do in a similar role outside of this company.

Even though there are additional engagement questions on a typical employee engagement survey, Culture Amp believes these five statements specifically are the foundation for measuring employee engagement.[15] Research from the Great Place to Work (GPTW) Institute reveals that engaged employees lead to higher performing organizations.[16]

To increase my credibility, I began using data to make better people-related decisions. I launched employee engagement surveys each quarter to measure employee sentiments around specific topics like leadership, collaboration, and rewards among other categories. These surveys allowed me to create metrics and goals and gave me a way to measure the impact of our people programs. When I studied the results of each engagement survey, I was relieved when the data clearly showed that the experience of working in tech for anyone other than a White male was at least 10–15 points lower in almost every single dimension of the engagement categories. I saw the same results across multiple companies, and it was

---

15   Ibid

16   Catherine Yoshimoto and Ed Frauenheim, "The Best Companies to Work for Are Beating the Market," *Fortune, February 27, 2018.*

the first time I had an accurate metric tied to what I had been seeing and sensing for so long.

In the fall of one particular year, one of the companies where I worked scored in the 90s (out of 100) on employee engagement. I knew we had a healthy business and a strong culture, and I wanted this company to gain public recognition. Thus, I took our results and applied to the GPTW contest. Every year, GPTW and *Fortune* magazine work together to publish a list of the best places to work. All companies are certified to place on this list based on the results of their engagement scores. That year, we won an award for being one of the one hundred best places to work in the United States.

#Winning

Since we won such a prestigious award, we had eleven people from GPTW come into our workplace to study our culture. They spent the morning with us and presented their thoughts on employee engagement at our all-hands meeting.

For our all-hands meeting, we had a jam-packed session of our normal agenda topics. We carved out twenty minutes from our programming and turned the microphone over to our guest speaker, Sally from GPTW. I could tell she was visibly nervous. She had prepared a slide show and started speaking about our scores, the results of what she noticed after spending some time with our company, and employee engagement in general.

I learned that only 30 percent of US employees are engaged in their companies, which leads to $450–$550 billion in losses for US-based employers each year.[17] [18] At the end of her presentation, Sally fielded some questions from the audience.

Afterward, I thanked her for her presentation. I could tell she was glad that the presentation was over, so I asked her a general question: "How do you think it went?"

Sally replied, "That was the first time that I've presented to *that* many men in one room." I acknowledged her trepidation and told her that she did a fine job and that, honestly, the audience appreciated her insights no matter the makeup of the crowd.

I wasn't sure why I uttered that sentiment.

Then it hit me.

I'd gotten so used to working with men that I didn't even notice that I was one of the few women, and one of the only minorities, who sat in the company, much less at the executive level. I had presented at the same all-hands meetings each week for years and failed to see who was in the audience.

---

17 Jim Harter, "U.S. Employee Engagement Hits New High after Historic Drop," Gallup, July, 22, 2021.

18 Kelly Wong, "10 Shocking Stats on Employee Disengagement," *Achievers* (blog), July 9, 2019.

I had two data points now: my daughter's comment about why I work with so many men and another aha moment from Sally presenting to a mostly male audience.

Even though I knew tackling the gender dynamic in tech was reported on and talked about, I still believed I could somehow make my companies be the heroes of the story by finally making it an inclusive place for women.

I interviewed a product leader for this book who led a cross-functional team of engineers, and she explained, "I was the leader of a product team, and male peers and executives didn't listen to me." She continued, "If a male on my team spoke, then they would listen to him before they listened to me. The men I worked with presented with a bravado that made me even question if they knew more than I did." Her advice about working in tech: "Realize that life is short. Don't be defined by what you do. I want to give myself permission to aim for happiness and balance rather than a title and prestige. In the end, I hope to surround myself with people who make that possible." Beth ended up shifting down in her career completely. She admits, "I've downgraded and actively removed myself from leadership roles when I can. I'm working on getting out of tech because I don't see a future in it for me, and it's not bringing me joy."

Amanda, a well-regarded HR leader in the tech scene who specifically asked me not to use her real name, shared, "I once went to a board meeting where I knew every board member yet was asked by one of the men to get him a cup of coffee." She explained, "I had to ask one of our recruiters to help me make a cup of coffee since I didn't even know how to use the machine. We made the cup of coffee, and I brought it back to him, sitting as the only woman in that board room that day." Years later, she mentioned that incident to her CEO, who said,

"I had no idea that even happened. Why did you bring him the coffee?" Flabbergasted, she replied, "We had to put our best foot forward that day, and although it made me feel like sh*t, someone had to do it." The CEO tried to apologize for not even noticing that the incident happened. It was not the only time Amanda felt others looking at her when asking about food or drinks in meetings filled with mostly men.

Companies try their best to find diverse talent to fill their most senior roles to serve as an example of how they want to be the change they wish to see in the world. They are all trying, although I believe we all still have a long way to go.

I interviewed an HR colleague, Erin, who worked in a leading news organization, about her experience trying to hire a chief technology officer (CTO) for the organization.

She describes the experience of being in a meeting to give an update on the CTO search. In a jam-packed room of hundreds of employees, the chief digital officer (CDO) proclaimed, "We are making solid progress on finding our new CTO. We've seen at least twenty strong candidates in these last few months. We hope to reach the offer stage within the next two weeks." A single hand shot up amidst the sea of employees gathered in the largest conference room in the fancy office space. With the sudden lone hand in the air, the CDO fielded the question. "How many of these potential CTO candidates are women?"

Stunned, the CDO flubbed with a nonanswer. The employees realized that in the sea of candidates, none of them were women. It was the first time the CDO even thought about it.

In her company, that moment awakened something for several women, who organized a task force to focus on hiring, retaining, and developing more women in technology. One of the programs they launched was a mentorship program where senior leaders would mentor rising female and minority professionals. Programs like these are hard to stand up and harder still to maintain. Of the many challenges they faced, they had many White men in the organization who felt uncomfortable grabbing coffee with women (for fear of the optics of meeting with young women) and diverse folks (with whom they had nothing in common). To launch the program, the task force addressed all of the concerns and codified all of the solutions in the program guidelines: Coffees would be in the cafeteria and paid for by sponsors; the program was mentee led, which meant meetings were scheduled by mentees; and there was a structure for each session. The task force learned a lot in their first mentorship pilot which had over one hundred participants. The program still exists today and was a success as it led to greater visibility and mobility for several participants. When Erin thinks back on her time, she laments, "I wonder what would have been possible if some of the men had taken more active roles, and we hadn't allowed them to be passive participants."

To improve the experience of being the only woman or the only minority at the table in my companies, I launched compensation studies to ensure we were paying women and minorities as much as their White male counterparts in every function. I hosted lunch and learn sessions about diversity and why it all matters (Hint: Diverse teams drive better business results).[19] I talked to my executive leaders and peers about what it felt like to be the "only" at their table (Spoiler alert: It sucked).

_____

19   Vivian Hunt, Dennis Layton, and Sarah Prince, "Why Diversity Matters," McKinsey & Company, January 1, 2015.

I took my role as an HR leader and slightly pivoted my focus to lean toward diversity, inclusion, and belonging (DIB). I did this because I knew all too well the emotions of loneliness and isolation from being the "only" at the table. I believed I could move the needle faster on propelling women and people of color to the top of an organizational pyramid by paying closer attention to these moments of isolation and calling them out by name. I had another more selfish reason to try to tackle DIB too: Emma, my twelve-year-old daughter, was going to enter the workplace in about ten years, so I was motivated to ensure that her executive table didn't look like mine always did.

As part of my self-empowered DIB charter, I wanted to expose White men to movies, books, and forums outside of their normal privileged, homogenous tech circles. I hosted unconscious bias trainings which teach us to see that we are the sum of all of our experiences and carry with us certain biases without recognizing them. These trainings ideally help us identify and mitigate bias so they don't negatively influence the way we hire, promote, or interact with colleagues. My CEO attended for the full two-hour session one Thursday morning. I was proud of him for showing up to learn and support this type of leadership training.

The problem was he showed up as the class clown who challenged everything that the speaker said without any regard for his tone or word choice. Fortunately, the speaker had a lot of experience dealing with those members in the audience who probably roll their eyes at her content and took all his comments in stride moving along the discussion quickly.

I still recall my CEO asking, "Why is it that men move around the furniture at work? Is that biased?"

While he may have thought his question was deep and clever, his tone and method of delivery made me want to slap him. Luckily, I composed my thoughts and told him here at Company X, Amy and Clare assemble office equipment and move it around each week, so it's the women who are breaking the gender stereotype. He smirked at me while the rest of the audience laughed knowing full well that indeed Amy and Clare did all sorts of operational things, including move furniture.

When Women's History Month arrived, I arranged a lunch meeting with the CEO and all the women at one of my companies. My aim was to shed light on what it felt like to be a woman in tech and a woman at that specific company. I gave the women some prompts to prepare for the meeting a week in advance. My intent was to host this session as a way to empower women to tell their stories and speak up about everyday life at Company X. I offered prompts like:

- What is it like to be a woman at this company?
- Do you feel you can contribute to conversations or meetings safely?
- What can we do to become more inclusive here at Company X?

I sent emails and instant messages via Slack to certain individuals who I knew had experienced gender bias at the company and asked them to contribute openly to the session.

The meeting day arrived, and the women spoke highly of our culture, which was good but did not surface any of the true microaggressions that occur daily. Our CEO had to actually admit that he knew about the all-male channels in Slack which excluded women. I could tell the women felt uncomfortable discussing this topic. Even when I had prompted them days before the meeting, they did not speak clearly about why those channels were offensive and exclusionary. I was disappointed knowing that they could not speak about their true emotions and experiences.

I could not understand why I felt so lonely at the top, and now here were more data points that led me to believe that I was alone in my fight. Even after preparing the women to talk openly about the male-dominated culture of our company, they had no words or stories to disclose. I could not rely or depend on anyone else to propel women, minorities, LGBTQ+ individuals, and other diverse employees to positions of leadership.

It was my uphill battle to fight, but I would fight hard knowing that I was working to show Emma that the world (and executive tables) could change.

Working in a tech start-up as a woman and a minority were two dimensions of who I was at work. I also had a third dimension: working parent. This last dimension, I believe, was the most important one to me, which is why I chose to stay in start-up life even after enduring all the abuse, gaslighting, and neglect.

I had Emma when I worked at one of my first tech start-ups. I loved the flexibility, freedom, and empathy that came from working in a fast-paced environment that understood that people also have a life outside of work.

At the time, I was working for a company that had just rolled out a brand new perk for all employees—unlimited vacation time. You read that right. Back in the early 2000s, tech companies began offering this incentive to their workers to try and boost morale and recruit new, hard-to-find talent. They figured that employees would perform better if they had the time they needed to rest and relax. While this idea sounded crazy at first, it quickly caught on once the research began to show that self-care helps employees increase productivity and avoid burnout.[20]

Emma had noon theater performances, after-school volleyball games, and parent-teacher conferences through the year, and at any time, I could let my team know and could be present at every event. The freedom and flexibility my companies gave to me would be one of the many reasons that made me stay in tech.

I tried to remain loyal when the company afforded me the flexibility to be there for the moments with my family that mattered the most. Nothing was better than shooting videos of her performances and being able to show up live and in the front row. I felt bad for those parents who were stuck in jobs where they had to calculate how to use their fifteen days of vacation throughout the year. I still remember Emma waving to me during her kindergarten graduation ceremony as she crossed the stage to receive her diploma. I smile looking back at that moment. For me, I work hard for Emma, and I was always present when she needed me on these special occasions.

---

20 Susan Biali Haas, "Forget Those Long Hours: Self-Care Drives Success," *Psychology Today, September 19, 2018.*

At Emma's kindergarten graduation ceremony. I tried to always get a front-row seat to Emma's various events,

Working in tech allows me to balance taking care of Emma with my busy work schedule. Tech companies allow you to have more freedom with less traditional working hours. The social contract is that with that freedom comes the obligation to work long hours, sign on to check emails even while on vacation, and address questions when the kids are asleep bed after hours. If you have responsibilities outside of work, if you like to volunteer your time during work hours, or if you define yourself beyond what you do for a living, you should consider working in a tech company.

The freedom and empowerment I feel from working for these tech companies is the reason why I stay in them. I know that the experience as a woman or minority in tech means that we must endure some of those moments that make us question if we're the only adults in the room. I know and have experienced the darker side of being the "only" flying solo at the executive table, but it was outweighed by my need to be a working parent who was present in Emma's everyday life.

I sacrificed my compass so that I could prioritize my life as a working parent. It was a choice I had to make. I had hope that there would come a time when I could be in a unique position to disrupt the power structures that exist throughout the workplace.

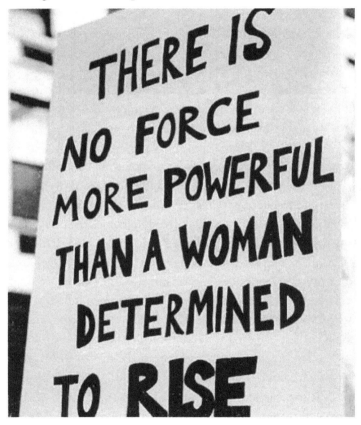

Preach!

PART 2

HATE TO LOVE

CHAPTER 9

ON PERKS AND PRIVILEGES

———

Have you ever seen the inside of a tech start-up? For those of you who have never been inside the halls of a tech start-up, let me give you a sense of the standard employee offerings.

The early generation of tech start-ups started the trend of offering perks that took care of employees' personal needs. It was the age of a highly competitive talent market, especially out in Silicon Valley where the war for talent created an arms race.

Companies offered all sorts of benefits to employees in order to attract them and keep them. My husband worked at Yahoo! and eBay in the early days where breakfast, lunch, and dinner were offered seven days a week. Haircuts, car washes, immunizations, dentist appointments, on-site dry cleaning, and personal trainers were available on demand whenever they needed. It was the heyday of tech companies blowing through budgets in service of their employees. While most companies attract new talent with sign-on bonuses, relocation packages, and sky-high salaries, elite tech companies offer those things and additional perks like sleep deprivation experts, personal chefs, and nutrition experts. Some companies even have cafeterias with chefs trained from private culinary institutes. Yelp has in-house baristas who make your favorite drink while Airbnb offers ten flavors of kombucha on tap and a lovely assortment of chef-inspired flavored waters.[21]

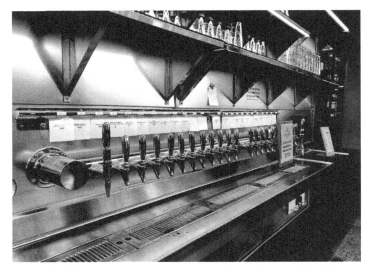

Oh the perks of working in start-ups. Fifteen flavors of iced kombucha on tap!

These latest perks are a small sample of what employees consider standard in start-up tech companies today. If you want to lure talent away from their current companies, you must provide a suite of perks to sweeten the offer package. It's become commonplace for employees to expect some of these benefits as table stakes. All the perks available in the first

---

21   Paul Schrodt, "12 Companies with the Most Luxurious Employee Perks," *Money, October 9, 2017.*

decade of the twenty-first century were no longer enough, and now companies needed to one-up each other. To win the talent war, tech start-ups evolved their benefits to put forward some of the most extreme perks the world has ever seen: on-site spas and therapists, unlimited vacation and extensive parental leave time, executive coaches, free legal services, egg freezing stipends, and IVF coverage. The list is extensive. A "best companies for employee benefits and perks" list actually exists where they rank the top twenty companies that provide the best perks, which feels like a whole other level of competition.[22]

To keep up with the competition, and because I wanted to show our employees that we cared about their health, we provided a Fitbit watch to every single person in our company. Less than 10 percent of our employees ever took sick days. I was worried that lunches at our desks, long working hours, and the high stress of working in a fast-paced environment was taking a massive toll on our employees.

I even remember my twenty-seven-year-old colleague Paul sharing that his doctor prescribed vitamin D because he wasn't getting enough sunlight in his life; it must have been the ten plus hour days at his desk. Scientists even coined the phrase "sunshine vitamin" and traced a deficiency in vitamin D to working in certain occupations.[23]

I brought in nutritionists to teach us how to cook with whatever food items we had in our homes; I provided specialists on-site who measured body mass index scores and

---

22 Richard Parris, "20 Best Companies for Employee Benefits and Perks," Tech.co, May 13, 2020.

23 Steven Reinberg, "Could Your Office Job Rob You of Vitamin D?" Medical Xpress, June 22, 2017.

nurses who drew blood to screen for diabetes, cholesterol, and high blood pressure. The results showed that a third of our population was prediabetic, most of them had high levels of the wrong cholesterol, and their stress levels were off the charts. The Fitbit was the quickest way to remind them that they needed to take care of their health. They appreciated the gesture and thought it was cool.

One will find amazing perks that are not advertised, and these are the perks that kept me in start-ups for as long as I can remember. For example, traveling while working in a start-up was a wonderful experience for me. Although every company has different travel policies, I was afforded the chance to explore the world as an ambassador for the companies I represented. I cannot explain how grateful I am to constantly have this opportunity.

I remember flying business class on an international flight to Sweden from San Francisco. It was the first time I ever flew "fancy." The reclining seats were a luxury, especially on a sixteen-hour flight overseas. The flight attendants in business class would constantly ask questions about food, beverages, snacks, and comfort. It was a totally different experience than flying coach.

I felt elitist entering through a different door in the plane and having flight attendants offer to hang up my coat and stow away my bags as soon as I stepped foot into the coveted front cabin. I sipped champagne even before the plane was in the air. I felt strange and out of place, honestly.

Without the generous policy of my company, I'm pretty sure I would never pay for this privilege myself. Luckily, my company had a policy of offering an upgrade for flights longer than ten hours. In all the companies where I worked, I visited all my employees in all the different offices around the world.

I visited London at least twice a year and made it to Sweden, Germany, France, Japan, and Italy as well as various domestic cities all throughout the United States.

I loved EVERY SINGLE moment of those visits that gave me a change of scenery from the monotony of my daily work routine. On many occasions, I was able to coordinate my flights with my husband's work schedule and Emma's school schedule so that we could travel as a family to see these fabulous destinations together. We explored the world together while I worked. I even had daycares in each of these cities that could watch Emma for the days when I needed to work in the office.

Annual trips to Paris and London with Emma

The list of benefits and perks was endless. It was awesome to be a part of a company and industry where they truly took care of all your needs outside of work. I benefited from all these perks. I had unlimited vacation time so I was able to take some time off whenever I needed. I had learning and development stipends, allowing me to take courses at the local college. I had wellness, bicycle, and various apps for free. I had the ability to travel and explore the world visiting the countries where we had offices. Even though I loved these lavish perks, I knew I would struggle at some point to manage employees' expectations. The perks war still rages on throughout Silicon Valley and has now transcended to other, more traditional companies. [24]

I believe the fringe benefits of working in tech start-ups is what kept me fighting the good fight on the harder days. Those big and small perks buoyed my spirits most days.

---

24 Leslie Barrie, "Wellness Perks Aren't Just a Draw for Silicon Valley Jobs Anymore," Skift, March 28, 2019.

Although no one uses it today, the Google slide is hard to miss

A beautifully designed working space for all the Airbnb employees in San Francisco

The Facebook Arcade

Time for a quick break at LinkedIn

An open space for eating while working

The plentiful bounty of food and drinks in tech start-ups

The lovely patio at one of the many Google buildings in Mountain View, CA

CHAPTER 10

JIMMY CHOOS

———

In the winter, I began working for a venture-based technology start-up in the San Francisco Bay Area—my fourth tech company. I came in as their first people leader.

I had to build the team, build the operational flow, and generally create all the different programs for the people function. I led a team that managed all the learning and development programs; I selected the HR tools and systems for every process flow at the company and handled compensation, benefits, and recognition programs. Typically, HR teams run lean and mean since most of the hiring budgets go toward sales and engineering. We had plenty of projects to tackle from start to finish, and we sometimes only had three people on the team.

I was the first senior level HR person to join the team, and I had to quickly learn how to map out my own priorities. We had a good product that was selling itself, we managed to double our revenue and our headcount in this particular year, and we were all running at breakneck speed. In the fast-paced life of Silicon Valley, we knew we didn't have enough people on our team, so we spent a full year hiring as many people as we could.

Across the company, we hired 130 people in the span of ten months. We had no performance review process, no compensation banding, no formalized IT department, and no formalized onboarding sessions amidst an incomplete executive team and a bunch of entitled and demanding employees. The average age of our employee base was only thirty-two, and the average tenure of our employee base was just under one year. We had a lot of new talent and not much structure. Who was allowed to have company credit cards? Who was in charge of managing the newly formed team of data scientists? The magic line became anyone vice president or above would get a company credit card for a random, yet logical, baseline. The reporting lines and the team structures of the company morphed each month depending on the series of jigsaw pieces in motion because we were hiring so many people. It didn't help that we were also losing some employees due to turnover. It was a thrill to complete the puzzle with a ton of moving pieces that didn't quite fit together, but the change was constant and the pace frenetic. Everything in a tech start-up is a work in progress.

I love being able to build from scratch. It is my life's work and my sweet spot. In a constantly changing work environment, you have to adapt all the internal operations to optimize people's productivity. HR teams do not build to create bureaucracy; instead, we build frameworks for decision making, allowing people to do their work more effectively.

For instance, if you want to give your direct report a raise or promotion, we have a template that a manager has to complete where they write a business case for it and then route it through emails to finance for approvals—nothing too onerous but much better than an ad hoc method. This particular company did not have an organized system for a performance review cycle; instead, they granted raises on the anniversary dates of each employee and promoted people whenever their role expanded or increased in scope or level. This is the constant jigsaw puzzle of operating in a business that has no internal infrastructure yet a ton of moving parts. New hires, constant exits, new teams, and frequent reorganizations driven by a new business strategy or a new revenue stream are just a few of the examples of what makes working in a start-up thrilling as well as exhausting.

For HR professionals like me who work in tech companies, we innovate process flows in order to build smooth operations. We don't take practices from traditional companies since the size and scale of these tech companies are different in scope. Plus, many employees wear different hats while a company is growing, thus making it difficult to set broad and stringent processes. Add in the tectonic shifts in the company, and we have to create our own rules and systems without trying to reinvent the wheel too much. We work hard and tirelessly to launch programs and processes that tackle a whole host of what is referred to as "organizational debt." Steve Blank, who spent twenty-one years in eight technology companies, describes organizational debt as "all the people/culture compromises made to 'just get it done' in the early stages of a start-up."[25] My team and I were busy setting up the systems and processes to optimize our operational flows. Our hope was to make sure the trains (in this case, the HR operations) were all running on time, making all the stops, and never breaking down.

---

25 Steve Blank, "Organizational Debt Is like Technical Debt—but Worse," *Steve Blank (blog), May 19, 2015.*

One day, I encountered a twenty-six-year-old that changed the way I thought about my work.

I met Jenny.

Jenny was a sales development representative (SDR). She graduated from college about three years prior to working for our company and wanted to try on sales as a career. She was young, well-spoken, and wore couture clothing even though she spent her days cold calling prospective customers from a cubicle.

SDRs earn good money since they have a base salary *and* earn a commission from every call that they can convert into an actual meeting. It's a tough job that requires an exceptional amount of grit to handle the constant rejection with the additional pressure of trying to meet a sales quota every quarter.

It was quarter three, and Jenny hit her sales numbers. She was excited since she was relatively new to the team. As part of the internal celebration, we posted names of all the employees who hit their quota for the month. After the celebration, I approached Jenny.

"Hi Jenny, congratulations on hitting your quota this month. I'm excited for you," I said.

Jenny responded, "I'm so excited, I'm going shopping at Saks tonight to get myself a pair of Jimmy Choo shoes." I looked at her with a mix of pride and confusion. I tried not to show it.

Jimmy Choo shoes

I was happy that Jenny was treating herself to a nice gift, but I was also worried as I knew that just last week, she had asked the company for a loan. Her stylish wardrobe came at a price, and although she looked polished and professional, I knew her financial priorities needed attention.

The next day, Jenny was wearing her brand-new, $700 Jimmy Choo high heels. "I like your shoes Jenny," I shouted out as I walked by her cubicle and smiled.

I can't understand the buying habits of sales professionals who earn commissions that are unpredictable, but knowing that Jenny spent a majority of her commission check on a pair of shoes *and* wasn't paying down her debt spurred me to bring in financial advisors to help our employees manage their money better.

That following month, financial advisors hosted a presentation on debt management and gave us advice about which bills to pay off first. During that presentation, I remember one of our employees, Sam, paying off her credit card on the spot. She was proud of herself and commented out loud, "I just paid off my credit card!"

The presenter was in shock, saying it was the first time that anyone had taken his advice while he was still presenting. The advisor exclaimed, "Wow, tech companies have people like Sam who learn fast and act quickly. It's so different from where I work."

Before I met Jenny, I was happy with all my good work allowing employees to use systems and processes that were simple, were easy to understand, and never broke down. Now after meeting Jenny and reflecting on Sam's desire to pay off her debt, I realized that my debt management presentations unlocked others. I still feel proud of my impact as an HR leader in moments like these.

All of the CEOs I've worked for fully empowered me to take care of employees. I found creative ways to offer perks that you wouldn't normally see in a small-size company. Not only did I bring in financial advisors, but I introduced wills and trust attorneys, life insurance experts, and even personal coaches and trainers who could help our employees take better care of themselves. My job was to ensure employees didn't have to deal with life's distractions so that they could do good work and to make their work worth the sacrifice of being away from friends and family each day.

Wonderful moments like this, I think, can only be found in these magical places we call start-ups. The days of working in a start-up offer a variety and cornucopia of workflows that stretch even the best critical thinkers.

The freedom and flexibility to do what was right for employees and the weight of my impact are some of the top reasons that I stayed in tech for as long as I did.

CHAPTER 11

CONTINUOUS LEARNING

———

I worked with a CEO who would spend hours pressing the space key to get the letters evenly spaced on a slide to be aesthetically pleasing to the audience. I worked with a lawyer who used to cajole me into using semicolons as a way to show depth in my storytelling abilities. I had one CEO urge me to think deeply about the future even though fires were brewing in the present. They all pushed me beyond the limits I imposed on myself. Working next to these types of leaders made me realize the importance of self-development and continuous learning.

Working in start-up tech companies isn't for everyone; many people think working in tech is sexy and fun with ping-pong or foosball tables and with rows of organic snacks and cereal lining the kitchen shelves. While many companies have these types of perks making an office feel like home, the boundaries of a tech company can feel very ambiguous.

One of my colleagues, Rick, used to work long hours and treat the office like his home. He left his toothbrush, shaving cream, and vitamins displayed neatly on his desk as if he was at home in his own bedroom. You were always "on" in tech, even if you were taking a vacation or even trying to sleep.

Work-life balance seemed to blur if you weren't careful managing your professional and personal lives. The flexible hours were expected, with colleagues sending an email, text, or Slack message at all hours of the day and night. The fact that colleagues responded to your own requests instantly meant that you owed them that courtesy to respond instantly too.

I spoke to Daniel, a serial HR leader for many tech companies. He said, "Building a start-up can feel like a race for survival. You build, learn, and improve because if you're not growing the business, chances are you won't survive for long. Some people live for that feeling; they thrive because passion to solve problems is their motivation. They refuse to fail. Most people however are risk averse, choosing to pursue outcomes with low uncertainty. The feeling of teetering on the edge between failure and greatness can be scary. Absolutely exhilarating, but not sustainable for most people."

Depending on the stage of the start-up, employees can wear many different hats. This means that one person can play the role of many different people in the company, especially for the harder-to-find skills.

For example, one of my CEOs played the role of chief financial officer (CFO), chief operating officer (COO), and CEO for at least three quarters before he hired for those unique positions. An engineering leader was also in charge of product marketing. Sometimes these employees loved wearing multiple hats. It allowed them to stretch their careers and abilities in challenging new ways. From the outside, it may look astonishing, but it becomes particularly messy when you can't rely on a given person to complete the plethora of tasks and projects asked of them.

This leads to an accountability problem. It's hard to fire the one person who's playing multiple roles because their attention is divided or scattered. They are trying to execute their tasks, although, realistically, they have too many things on their plate to finish projects, much less do them well. This gray area makes working in tech hard to stomach. Everyone wants to make an impact and do good work; everyone suffers when they can't.

Working in this gray space of not knowing where your role starts or ends defines some of the moments that make working in tech difficult. Some people do not operate well in this space of ambiguity, having to flex around one person who happens to be in charge of multiple different dimensions. It is one of the many reasons why tech companies suffer from volatile retention rates, with the average employee leaving the company in only three years. Employees simply can't keep up with the volume of work or, worse, grow exhausted from switching contexts all day long.[26]

For me, I played the role of HR leader, mapping out the people strategy for the entire company. I taught sessions as a coach and trainer for all leaders in the company; I managed the budgets for the real estate and made all decisions related to the office space; I planned all the summer and holiday parties to boost morale; I chose charitable causes to donate to with time or money; I managed IT; and one of the best things about my job was that I became the unlicensed therapist to the CEO. I had a set of expansive responsibilities that never ended. I relished handling all those opportunities since I learned a ton from having to figure things out myself.

My role never came with an onboarding kit or playbook. I had to create the programs and execute them with sometimes

---

26   Paula Clapon, "Can the Tech Industry Solve the Employee Tenure Problem?" Hppy, accessed on February 9, 2021.

only teams of two or three people. All of this work took place in conjunction with managing and leading HR teams through various stages of growth. My days were varied and I loved learning new things. To this day, I think if you stay curious and take on as much responsibility as you can, you become a more valued and crucial employee.

Those roles and responsibilities are now part of my toolkit. I spent fifteen years building this toolkit and knowing how to be a Swiss Army knife at a moment's notice. Despite the ambiguity of my role and all the hiring and churn around me, I had the chance to sit on executive teams at a young age. If I would have stayed in some of my previous careers, I don't believe I would have made it to the executive teams in as fast a time as I did. I learned to be a part of the Silicon Valley tech scene, learning how to think as an HR leader in order to bring out the best in people. I've had many people take chances on me, including the banker I mentioned earlier in the book, the CEOs who entrusted me with their deepest secrets or fears, and the various teams I've had the pleasure to serve.

Tech companies distinguish themselves from the traditional corporate companies by taking more risks. In Facebook's early days, they posted the mantra "What would you do if you knew you weren't afraid?" all over their headquarters. Most tech companies disrupt some aspect of a traditional business and take chances with developing leaders who may not have the requisite experience. Most of the CEOs I worked with were in the age range of 32-42, so they were quite young. Some of them had never had a job other than being the cofounder of their own tech start-up. These same CEOs took a risk on me by giving me a seat at the executive table even though I hadn't amassed a ton of experience in the

HR world myself. Some days I knew I was out of my element and out of my comfort zone, while other days, I could piece together what I needed to do and knew that it was okay to try and fail.

Beverly, who we met in previous chapters, believes the same thing: People in start-ups can experience rapid success with a blank canvas from which to build a team, a product, or even a company.

Amanda, the HR leader who served the cup of coffee to her board member, explained that in some companies, they tend to have a strong bias for recruiting people who went to Ivy League schools. Her recruiting team was falling into the same trap of competing for the same talent pool from the same schools. Amanda encouraged her team to find people from nontraditional paths and backgrounds to help make the company more diverse. Having earned her undergraduate degree from an unknown university and then an MBA from a well-regarded school, she knows firsthand the doors that opened for her because she had an institutional connection. Through her own abilities to spot some unconscious patterns, Amanda made sure that her company's own recruiting practices buck the trend of tech start-ups' propensity to build homogenous teams.

Amanda's story epitomizes the best thing about working in start-ups. These ecosystems allow you to learn as you go; you can identify old habits and change them on the fly.

I interviewed Melanie, a three-time HR leader, who shared her love for building, learning from her employees, and iterating quickly at a start-up. "We run weekly stand-up meetings (similar to what a product or engineering team may do) where we review our goals and potential blockers to achieving them." She continued, "We roll quickly, and we're always iterating, which means we are constantly getting feedback and learning. Shipping something 80 percent finished is common. We then continue to learn from our employees to tweak the other 20 percent over time which ultimately gets us to a better product in the end. This iteration and learning is what makes our work fun!"

It is one of the greatest joys of working in tech; you get to work with interesting and sometimes inexperienced yet curious people to build something great. Everyone has a unique opportunity to grow and shine. Start-ups' tolerance for risk is what defines them as a unique work environment. No one hovers or micromanages you. You must be self-motivated to accomplish what you set out to do daily. No one will hold your hand or guide you in this start-up life. It's both scary and exhilarating at the same time!

Working in a start-up *is* a lot of work. It can be overwhelming, and it's important for people to recognize when it's too much for them and when the culture isn't quite right. Leading multiple, disparate projects and building the infrastructure for a company as you go is like being thrown into the deep end of the pool and learning how to swim: You force yourself to figure it out fast.

Rick's display of his bedroom didn't bother me in the end; I knew that his long hours meant that I would have to work my butt off too. His neat desk display signaled something more perverse for me: No one had work-life balance at that particular company. I only spotted this pattern after I burned myself out from working so hard.

Conversely, for those who like to take this kind of high-speed, ambiguous ride, it can be thrilling and rewarding every single day of your professional life. The greatest feeling is knowing that the work you do makes a drastic impact for everyone in a company.

To this day, I still try to stay curious and take on additional tasks by asking more questions and listening to the answers. We have two ears and one mouth for a reason.

CHAPTER 12

ON WORKING WITH MILLENNIALS

—

I've worked with many Generation Y employees, also known as millennials. According to The Center for Generational Kinetics, millennials are defined as America's youth born between 1977 and 1995.[27]

The average age for the companies I worked at was a mere thirty-two including, all executives. Once you removed executives, the average age would drop to twenty-nine. Most tech companies skew on the young side, choosing innovative disruptors over years of experience. In other words, the world of tech is dominated by millennials. I believe that younger CEOs, who are new to the CEO seat, hire people in their own networks, which generally means friends who run in their same professional and social circles. An *AngelList* blog post written in August of 2018 states that "early-stage employees,

---

27

The Center for Generational Kinetics, "Generational Breakdown: Info About All of the Generations," accessed February 25, 2020.

overall, are driven by high-risk, high-reward opportunities—a very different motivator than you might find in a later-stage hire."[28]

Most companies employ at least five generations in the workplace. According to The Center for Generational Kinetics, generations can be broken down into the following categories:

- The Silent Generation (or traditionalists) born before 1945
- Baby boomers born 1946–1964
- Generation X born 1965–1976
- Millennials (or Generation Y) born 1977–1995, and
- Generation Z born 1996–TBD[29]

There are many generational differences in the workplace. Many articles, like one from Paychex in 2019, have been written about how to build cohesion between these five different bases.[30] It is hard to build cohesion in a workplace that has employees of various age groups dealing with different phases of life. The issues that face a new college graduate trying to pay off student loan debt are very different from someone is calculating how much they need to set aside for their own retirement.

---

28 Caleb Kaiser, "How to Hire Your First 10 Employees," *AngelList Blog,* *August 17, 2018.*

29 The Center for Generational Kinetics, "Generational Breakdown."

30 Paychex, "How to Manage the 5 Generations in the Workplace," last modified July 26, 2019.

In 2016, the Pew Research Center published that millennials are the largest generation in the US population.[31] This holds true in the companies where I worked, as we mostly employed workers from Generation Y. This tendency to hire more young-ish workers made me focus on the career needs of a generation that is not shy about asking for raises, promotions, and new titles. Millennials shunned the idea of having to serve years in a role to gain credibility or experience; instead, they took on added responsibilities as a way to learn more and shared their dreams of wanting to be promoted to VP of X department despite having had little or no experience in management.

I remember an inside sales representative (ISR) who approached me. "My goal is to be a VP of sales in about two more years," Sean declared.

Sean had been born with a silver spoon in his mouth. He had a good family, a good education, and a good job, but none of that made him management material. Though he was the go-to person in his department, he lacked the leadership skills required of a VP. It also didn't help that he often acted as if life in our start-up was an extension of his college fraternity house—drinking at 4:00 p.m., coming in hungover, and even falling asleep during meetings.

I took a deep breath and looked at him, trying to keep my composure. This conversation was not going to be easy.

I inadvertently rolled my eyes at him. *How could he be this naive?*

In one of my most unfiltered moments, I told Sean that he wasn't ready and that just because he was the go-to person for

31   Richard Fry, "Millennials Are the Largest Generation in the U.S. Labor Force," Pew Research Center, April 11, 2018.

questions did not mean that he was leading a team. "Sorry to burst your bubble, Sean, but you have many things to learn that will take more than two years to develop."

It wasn't my most positive interaction with an employee. The belief among older generations is that many members of this coddled, everyone-wins-a-participation-trophy generation feel entitled. With that in mind, I felt the need to set expectations with Sean. I had to let him know that he had a long way to go and needed to humble his ego. I kept talking to avoid his response.

"I think you have more to learn. You should go and experience different-sized companies and teams and build more leadership muscles. VPs at this company are subject-matter experts in their domains, they go to conferences to speak about their craft, and they know how to manage and lead teams. Those all sound like easy things to do, yet I've seen many people struggle with managing people; it takes years to amass those skills and do them well."

I cringed waiting for his response since I knew this wasn't what he wanted to hear.

"Which of those management skills don't I have now?" Sean asked. "New hires come to me all the time to ask questions, so I believe I already manage people. I speak at our sales meetings to give lessons on how to sell, and I'm known as an expert on the team."

"Sean, training new hires is part of your job description. That doesn't make you management. And don't get me started on your 'speaking engagements.' While giving presentations to your own peers is a great start, it doesn't make you a subject-matter expert."

Sean looked down at his feet. It was the first time I had seen him lose that cocky confidence and become vulnerable.

After a moment, he looked back up and asked simply, "Well…
will you help me then?" I admired Sean's conviction to chart
his own career path, and I vowed to help him.

After many of these types of discussions, I realized I was
actually inspired by this millennial generation who thought
deeply about where their careers were going and how to get
there, even giving themselves a timeline to get to their goals.
From my experience, Gen Xers and baby boomers would
rarely try to pave their own course, choosing instead to take
whatever was offered after their many years of hard work and
effort. It was unusual to have Gen X or baby boomers ask for
promotions or raises; they were patient and took whatever
they got without complaint. An article written by Lindsey
Pollak, a career and workplace expert, reveals how certain
segments of the world even forget about Gen X altogether. [32]

Once I started to help Sean, I had other employees reach
out to me to set aside walks or coffee chats to pick my brain
about career options and mobility opportunities within our
own company. My millennial colleagues didn't have any fear
of asking for help and were brazen enough to think that they
had the skills necessary to rise quickly.

I loved that part of working with them.

Later, these chats would inspire me to build programs
that trained employees to understand their blind spots and
lead fulfilling lives where they could develop a clear path to
their goals. I taught ways to understand their own strengths,
acknowledge their development areas, and put a plan together
to get where they wanted to go in their careers. Through a

---

32 Lindsey Pollak, "Gen X, the Forgotten Middle Child: Is It Any Wonder
That Our Theme Song Is 'Don't You Forget about Me?'" *Lindsey Pollock
(blog), September 9, 2019.*

ton of self-awareness and reflection exercises, my employees began to understand how to align their efforts toward their own stated goals.

To this day, I love that they knew what they wanted. It was my job to help them get there. Working in HR and in tech start-ups has some fabulous moments like these. The impact that I have on individual careers is rewarding, almost like seeing your own child walk for the first time or watching your team win as an underdog. These moments carried me through all the tougher moments of working in tech as an Asian woman who many underestimated purely because of my stature. Working with millennials made me feel young and made me smile; I would need these moments to buoy me for the rocky days ahead.

CHAPTER 13

BURNOUT

One weekend in May of 2018, I went shopping in San Francisco and roamed into one of the touristy shops that line Fisherman's Wharf. I found a small artistic shop that sold creative patches, socks, and all sorts of apparel. I found a simple, black baseball cap. It was nothing special, but I loved the patch on its bill: "No people today." I bought it and chuckled knowing that HR people and managers everywhere would understand that it takes a lot to manage employees. I believe that people are the most unpredictable part of any business.

I was exhausted and I hated my job. My performance was slipping, and I was working longer hours than I had ever in my life. I was burned out and going through the motions of doing my job but finding utterly no joy in doing so. The moments where I helped everyone else felt good, but no one was there to help me. I was burning out and not even realizing it. Now that I was experienced with all sorts of HR programs, I had lost my passion for my own profession. I was tired of being the one behind the scenes orchestrating the symphony.

The things that make us love something or someone are also the things that make us hate them. Only when I got out of serving in the role of HR leader could I see that juxtaposition. The World Health Organization (WHO) defines burnout as "feelings of energy depletion or exhaustion; increased mental distance from one's job, or feelings of negativism or cynicism related to one's job; and reduced professional efficacy."[33] Alternatively, but also related to burnout, WHO defines stress as "the response people may have when presented with work demands and pressures that are not matched to their knowledge and abilities and which challenge their ability to cope."[34] Burnout is different from stress. "Stress occurs in a wide range of work circumstances, yet is often made worse when employees feel they have little support from supervisors and colleagues, as well as little control over their work processes."[35]

I had both and didn't even know it.

It was fall, and I looked up one day in our beautiful office space. The space was professionally designed by an urban designer. We had custom-made furniture and used some combination of modern, functional pieces along with the sleek design lines of Herman Miller and Design Within Reach. In our conference rooms, we scattered nice wooden or marble tables along with the coveted Eames chairs. It was a nice blend of old and new with warm colors. We offered different types of spaces and furniture pieces for the many ways

---

33   World Health Organization, "Burn-Out an 'Occupational Phenomenon': International Classification of Diseases," May 28, 2019.

34   World Health Organization, "Occupational Health: Stress at the Workplace," 19 October, 2020.

35   Ibid.

that people need to work today. I love coming into spaces that are well designed and well proportioned since we generally spend at least nine hours a day at work. Might as well make the space inviting and beautiful.

I looked out on the open office layout and thought to myself, *Is this what I'm going to do for the rest of my life?* I have at least fifteen more years to work, and I couldn't figure out if I was happy doing what I did for nine hours each day, even if I did enjoy coming into the custom-designed office.

My brother and I planned to have dinner one night. I told him I wanted to treat him since I hadn't seen him in such a long time, and I asked him to choose the restaurant. After blurting out some choices, I told him, "Will you just pick one? I can eat anything."

He looked at me incredulously and said, "We're supposed to have a nice dinner and instead you ruin it by being combative." We didn't have dinner that night, and before he walked away, he told me that whatever I was doing at work was changing my personality and making me hard to be around.

We're influenced heavily by those who we spend time with. I knew I worked with teams who were argumentative, and I often had to be the HR person in the room facilitating dialogues and conversations between coworkers. That same combative tone was affecting my personal life.

When my friends and I would go out socially, they would ask me about work. My friend Virginia would ask me a simple question like "How's work?"

I always provided the same answer: "I really wish I could retire early and travel for a while."

My friends would tell me that this specific answer led them to believe that my dream of early retirement was me actually telling them that I was tired of my work. (Thank you, Virginia!)

To add one more truth, Virginia said, "Mai, your job hasn't brought you joy in a long time."

Other family members like my mother and even my husband saw me working long hours without much time or energy to truly enjoy life. I was working a full day, and after my daughter would go to bed, I would get back on my laptop to try to get ahead of the next day by catching up on emails and finalizing my projects. I had so much to do; I was working on ten projects at a time. All of them I delivered on time—all of them mediocre. I simply didn't have enough hours, so I sacrificed quality for quantity.

Even when I traveled to fabulous places for work, I couldn't find the time to explore or take in the sites of each city. I satisfied my love of travel, although work was constantly in the background haunting me. One morning while in London with my mother, I realized that I would have to work the entire day; London was nine hours ahead which meant that I would put in a full day in our London office and have to stay online once our San Francisco teams woke up. It was a grueling schedule.

That was the moment I realized that the job I was doing every day for at least nine hours a day wasn't bringing me joy at all. It was doing the opposite and making me mean, tired, and grouchy.

In hindsight, one of the main reasons for my burnout was that in the companies where I worked, we did not have budgets. Start-up land means you have to ask finance for money each time you want something. New tool? Ask finance. Want to outsource a true learning and development culture and hire some instructors? Go ask finance. Most of the CFOs

I worked for preferred not to have budgets since they felt creating budgets meant that leaders would simply use them up. The CFOs I knew reasoned that if they gave us *no* budget, then we would be more careful and thoughtful about whether or not we truly needed the thing. Try researching all the different tools missing and asking for budgets at least five times a month. It gets *really* old.

Since I never had an actual budget, I was never able to hire a complete HR team or have the authority to purchase a full suite of HR tools. I had to be the strategic HR visionary and also the executor of all of my ideas. This constant ping-pong of context switching and altitude drifting was something that I thought I loved. Over time, I realized that I was serving too many roles across the HR function. No one seemed to appreciate that I was doing so many things, not even me. I was on fire.

On my worst days, I would get annoyed if people came to me with problems and no solutions. I knew the average age of most of the leaders was thirty-two at most of the companies where I worked, but I forgot that some of them had no real-world experience and couldn't come to me with any solutions. They simply had no business tools yet.

On good days, I felt empowered to do my thing and focus on the ten projects I was working on; I felt a sense of pride in everything I rolled out. Younger, less experienced colleagues were thirsty to develop solutions that would further their own careers. I could use my influence across the company to help implement cool ideas that we invented ourselves. However, no amount of authority or empowerment could ease the sting of a bad day. I still remember one instance when we were at an executive meeting. I and two other female coworkers were sitting on the same side of the table when one of the leaders walked into the room, pointed a finger sharply at us and with a nonchalant tone said, "You three are invited to this meeting, but you are not allowed to talk."

Stunned and too tired to process the situation, I walked out of the room. The ability of grown adults to treat others like crap was really starting to gnaw at me like never before. This episode was even worse since it was rooted in misogyny. I thought to myself, *this isn't the company I joined.* I knew the most recent hires we made on the executive team changed the chemistry of the original company. I knew it was time for me to make a choice—stay and endure more days like this or leave and change my own circumstances.

I thought about constantly trying to keep up with the hundreds of emails per day, the two hundred Slack messages per day, and the constant stream of work that had me pivot from being HR strategist to leading manager trainings to preparing a slide presentation for the board of directors. It was exhausting work, and the constant context switching wore me out.

I would get off a phone call on which I was discussing one small detail about a tool with a vendor and then have to present at the all-company meeting on our goals for the quarter. I thought I loved how all this motion stretched my leadership capacity; in the end, it was all draining me.

As I was constantly spinning plates and running around to make sure none of them dropped and shattered, I was producing half-hearted, mediocre work. The learning and development sessions were becoming shortened lessons with lengthy interactive dialogues so that I didn't have to lead the full discussion. All the organic snacks were the same for three straight months because I was too busy to choose a different lineup of snacks. The holiday party was the same holiday party; I had simply changed the venue.

Some of these things are definitely first world start-up problems: Organic snacks, global holiday parties, and flying in employees outside the United States into headquarters are things you see in movies, yet it was the reality of my world. The weight of all these projects, big and small, was too overwhelming for me to care too much about the work I was producing. I didn't have the headspace to think about how I could make work awesome; my frame of mind was that "done" was good enough.

Toward the end of my start-up journey, that attitude didn't serve me well. As the job morphed into a confluence of roles and duties for me, I grew apart from my true passions—DIB, engagement, and creating world-class leaders. I couldn't devote the right amount of time to what I really cared about.

I left the tech start-up world, finally, after fifteen years of knowing nothing else. I took almost two years off from being an in-house HR leader and became an on-demand, gig economy worker.

During my newfound leisurely schedule, I wrote a Medium article and did an interview with Lars Schmidt, the host of a podcast called *21st Century HR*, to tell my story on burning out. [36] I spoke about my high-effort work and my fifteen-year journey with a seat at the executive table. I told stories about the crazy perks and the great moments of working in tech. My voice quivered when I talked about being

---

36   Mai Ton, "Burn(ed) out," Medium, *October 7, 2019.*

the only minority and only woman at the table struggling to be a role model for my twelve-year-old daughter, Emma.[37]

"I have ten years to move the needle faster on changing the face of the executive table for Emma's generation. They will be in the workforce in the year 2031 (assuming they go to college and graduate in about four years), and I worry that we still haven't made significant progress on making work healthier and more inclusive for them even though we've been trying to make tech more inclusive for decades."

I received such positive responses for admitting that I was struggling with my job that I finally felt like a weight had been lifted and I was no longer Sisyphus. Being vulnerable and asking for help, and finally having some time to reflect on my own choices and sacrifices finally led me to feel joyous for the first time in many years.

During these two years as a gig worker, I was able to truly understand what I wanted and what I was missing from the many places that I worked previously. I found focus. I also finally found the time to write this book.

Reading that the average tenure in the tech industry is a mere three years and that the tech industry has the highest rates of turnover gave me perspective that I wasn't alone in my struggles or my burnout.[38] [39] Many others were feeling the same way I did.

---

37   Mai Ton and Lars Schmidt, "Ep39 EMP HR Consulting Founder Mai Ton, Navigating Burnout in HR," November 11th, 2019, in *21st Century HR, produced by Lars Schmidt, podcast, MP3 audio, 24:18.*

38   Paula Clapon, "Can the Tech Industry Solve the Employee Tenure Problem?" Hppy, accessed on February 9, 2021.

39   Michael Booz, "These 3 Industries Have the Highest Talent Turnover Rates," *Linkedin Talent Blog, March 15, 2018.*

I talked to Myra, who is a repeat HR leader at start-ups that have year-over-year growth rates of 100 percent and who is responsible for all the heavy lifting to try to make HR operations function smoothly. When she was younger, it was easier to devote herself to the job; now with two kids, she has to reserve her energy for her family. She has been one of the lucky ones to experience a life-changing IPO, but she had to pay the price by working her butt off. When I asked her if all the years of hard work were worth it, she had to pause to answer the question.

She responded after careful reflection, "I probably hated it at the time, but I wouldn't change anything about my career. My life in tech start-ups gave me the chance to learn many elements of HR quickly. I don't think I could have learned so much in such a short period of time anywhere else."

I wish I could say the same. I was too tired to really understand how to look back and make it a positive reflection.

Even though I was burned out, I found hope in knowing that I could use my skills to help others in the HR community in some way. I took some time off, finally. After a quick month of no employment, I realized that I could propel other HR leaders to learn from me. I had many lessons to share, and instead of letting my own HR community make the same mistakes I did—take on too much, let offensive comments sit, be okay with the status quo, etc.—I would teach them my own lessons so that they wouldn't have to learn them the hard way. I had done the falling down for them; now it was my turn to share my thoughts so that they could see around the corners more quickly and anticipate HR matters better. I could do something with my skills that helped many, instead of always using my skills to help just one company at a time.

On May 22, 2019, I registered my business with the New York City county recorder, and I officially hung up a shingle on the internet. I was going to become an HR consultant to help the many HR leaders and companies that needed someone to parachute in and assist them with a variety of HR matters. It would become the first stepping stone in my journey to carve a new path.

I was nervous about leaving the steady income of a full-time, in-house job and trading it in for a chance to do something on my own. My newfound courage would give me a break from the routine of my last fifteen years and challenge me to explore an unknown, yet exciting, chapter ahead.

PART 3

LOVE CONQUERS ALL

CHAPTER 14

CONSULTING

———

Since I had fifteen years of experience in tech start-ups, I built my website to reflect that I thrived in particularly fast-paced, high-growth tech companies. I loved the idea of parachuting in and out of companies when they needed me, knowing that I could work on a variety of projects to keep me stimulated.

I joined more HR networks and started posting regularly to LinkedIn and even Instagram. I felt fortunate that I had built a network of colleagues who knew me. I spent days networking by conducting phone calls with people who encouraged me to talk with their friends who had started their own businesses. I even hired coaches to help me through this next phase of my professional life. I asked these mentors to provide me with the lessons they wished someone had taught them before they went out on their own. I had a specific lineup of questions about how to price my services, how to build a website, how to bill time, and how to create an invoice so that I could understand everything that I needed to know to build a successful business.

I had questions like:

1. How do I price my services—flat fee, project-based, or by hourly rate?
2. Do I really need a website to drive sales? Should pricing be disclosed on my website?
3. If charging by the hour, do you round up or down? By the fifteen-minute increment or thirty-minute increment?
4. Should I give some consulting hours for free to get clients through the door?

I remember one specific conversation with Jess, an HR leader who had a similar journey to me in that she worked in four different start-ups, was a working parent, and handled everything under the umbrella of HR strategy. We had our first phone call in the summer of 2018.

"You will love the freedom and independence of being out on your own since you can hop on calls from anywhere. Right now, I'm in Spain with my family, and we are going to the beach after we finish this call," she told me.

The thought of being able to lead a life of leisure and generally not feel the pressure from an in-house job where you must care about the entire organization and its people felt right for me. I could find harmony in earning an income AND jumping in and out of companies on my own timeline.

At this point in my life, I believed that spending time with Emma, who was only eleven years old then, was definitely a big part of why I needed more flexibility in my schedule. We spend so much time working as adults that I fear we are all missing out on the best parts of life. No one ever regrets missing that meeting at work as much as they regret missing that middle school play.

Jess continued, "The hardest part will be advising your clients to do one thing and them not doing anything that you advise. It took me some time to get used to that because I thought, *what's the point of hiring me if you aren't going to take my advice?*"

In the end, I provided customized outcomes and services even if they did not implement my recommendations. I shrugged my shoulders and still earned decent money from working the hours I wanted and got to choose which clients I worked with.

That summer, I outsourced my website to a gig worker to produce a website. I paid $25 for the work and $65 for the iconography on my site (www.emphrconsulting.com), and it only took one week to build. If I had tried to do this myself, I would have taken at least six months to build it. For me, this was money well spent, and this became my first lesson: If you aren't good at something, consider outsourcing it. There are many tools (Fiverr, Upwork, etc.) that allow you to spend your time on things you are good at and outsource the things you are not good at to more skilled professionals. Below are some of my favorite resources that helped me prioritize my time on my strengths.

Resources for Consultants

Business Needs	Resources
Websites - from start to finish	Fiverr or Upwork
Marketing - Branding, iconography, icons, and slogans	Your network of friends or Fiverr
Billing - Invoices, bills, and accounting	FreshBooks or Bill.com
Expenses related to the business	Expensify
Scheduling	Calendly or Doodle

One other benefit to being an independent consultant is that I earn more money working fewer hours with less stress than

I would by being employed in a company. I had control over my own time, could take calls and do work from anywhere, and could charge a high price tag for my years of experience. All these factors gave me the chance to earn more money flexing my hours up when I need more income or flexing down when I want more time for my personal pursuits (including the ability to write this book).

According to a *Harvard Business Review* study in conjunction with the consulting firm Eden McCallum and the London Business School, "Consultants' self-reported full-time equivalent salary information indicated that women are more fairly compensated once they go independent." Being an independent consultant allows for "greater control over their time and a better work-life balance [which] were the two key reasons women became independent."[40]

I made calls to and networked with others to pick their brains about how to sell my services each day before I felt comfortable launching my business. I took a break one day to attend a meeting with a New York people leaders network group where I met Melissa, who would become one of my first clients. We talked about our shared passion for all things HR and what type of projects I would be open to helping her with. With all my nerves, I replied, "Anything you need me to do, I'm on demand for you." The next week Melissa hired me for a simple recruiting project, and within the second month of my arrangement with her, she gave me even more responsibility; she unveiled her company's desire to divest from their parent company. It would become one of my first

---

40   Dena McCallum, Susan J. Ashford, and Brianna Barker Caza, "Why Consultants Quit Their Jobs to Go Independent," *Harvard Business Review,* July 15, 2019.

strategic projects that would last for eight months! Within two months of building my website, I was working forty plus hours a week and earning a steady (and decent) income.

Shortly thereafter, and within three months of launching my business and website, I found my second client through a friend. I was getting emails from my website, trying to understand how to sell myself, and spending time trying to find new clients when surprisingly, I got a call from my friend Christine.

We caught up with a little small talk, then she asked me, "Mai, do you do compensation? We need to understand if we are paying our employees competitively with market rates, and I thought of you. Can you help us with that, and can you take on any more clients?"

I spent twenty minutes with Christine on the phone discussing the finer details, and I was hired after that first call. All of a sudden, I had two clients in the span of three months. I started to believe *I can do this*.

I charged a flat fee based on how many hours I estimated it would take me to finish the compensation study. It was my second lesson on being out on my own: the ability to understand how to price an engagement. I could charge what I thought was fair to me yet charge businesses more for the depth and breadth of my years of experience. It would have taken them twice the amount of time to do what I did in less than two months. As the gig economy flourishes, companies are finding it less costly and more efficient to outsource certain projects. My advice if you ever want to try to have a side hustle is to take on a side project and charge a small amount to see how it feels. You will be surprised by the quick learnings yielded.

By the fall of 2019, I had two clients—one who had me working forty plus hours per week and another who needed me to handle a project from start to finish for a flat fee. Both clients kept me busy as though I was working full-time, although they both allowed me the time to set my own hours. I didn't start work at 9:00 a.m. every day; instead, I set my own hours, making sure to check in, communicate clearly, and stay on top of their own deadlines. Even though I had plenty of work with only two clients, I worried that I needed to add more clients to ensure a decent income for the next few months.

As a consultant, the hardest part is knowing when and where your next client will come from. Relying on your friends and network purely isn't enough; I knew I had to pitch my services to keep a steady stream of interest from prospective clients. I joined more networks, met more people through meetups, and generally became a roaming sales-woman. I was selling my own skills as services, so I knew if I could sell myself, then I would secure more work and more income. If I didn't close sales, I knew it would spell disaster for my own business.

I rarely had to flex a sales muscle in my body as a company's HR leader; now I had to flex it almost daily. Learning how to sell would be a newly acquired tool that I needed to learn how to use quickly.

The only sales I did in the past was to get buy-in from a CEO or CFO on a project or tool. I had no real-world selling chops. Now, I was on my own and had to learn quickly how to sell my services. I knew my specific areas of passion (DIB, coaching, and engagement); I could articulate what made me different from all the other HR consultants in the world—my specific experience in building the HR operations in high-growth tech start-ups; and I knew how to price my services. I needed to learn how to sell—and fast. I wanted to have more clients waiting in the wings in case my other clients' projects ended quickly or suddenly. I rarely felt in control of the forces that make businesses hire me one day and tell me that they don't need my services the next week. I applied pressure to my sales pipeline knowing that the rug could be pulled out from under me at any given moment.

I took two and half years to renew my passion for all things HR. I was finding my groove as a consultant. At one point I laughed at having to upgrade to a higher service plan on my billing platform because I had more than five clients, the maximum allowed in the basic plan I had purchased. I could feel a reset in my attitude and a shift in my mindset.

Me at the HPI HQ in Florida

I grew more curious about who I was and what I wanted. I took personality tests and purpose tests and went to the

Human Performance Institute (HPI) to define my mission in life. If you ever get the chance to visit HPI, you should. It is one of the most amazing experiences that finally gives you time to focus on yourself for a moment. They offer programs of different lengths that allow you to finally focus on uncovering *why* you work so hard. They train you to optimize your own performance by discovering the answer to the question: "What really drives your desire to work?" It takes a tremendous amount of self-reflection to respond fully to this one simple question. After attending the one-week program at HPI, I created a mission statement that anchors all my decisions on where I spend my time. Writing a mission statement was tough. This one sentence captures my hopes and ambitions for my refreshed way of thinking: My mission is to be an extraordinary person who is kind, compassionate, and optimistic so that I can bring out the extraordinary in others.

With my newfound zest for doing good work, I read hefty business and self-help books, talked to more people, and hired two career coaches to help me make sense of how to align my passions with how to earn an income. It's funny that the long hours, hefty projects, and emotional toll of working in HR for fifteen years culminated with me burning out, but this unhealthy state forced me to take a break and discover what I wanted to do with the rest of my working life. This unhealthy state forced me to take a break and discover what I wanted to do with the rest of my working life. I anchor everything I do in my own mission statement now and feel good knowing that I'm rooted in something more meaningful than just me.

I could not have reignited my love for HR without having taken some time off to reset. A midlife crisis can present itself in different ways for different people. Some may need excitement through purchasing a motorcycle, while others may prefer going to an ashram.[41]

For me, my midlife crisis was starting my own business. I believe that I am a much better person for having taken time off from working a traditional nine-to-five job. After experiencing burnout, I also believe that these last two and a half years have been the best years of my life as a working parent, mother, and wife. I feel less stressed and more focused and have harmony with the projects in both my professional and personal lives.

I never had the ability or time to devote to that level of thinking before, which I believe makes me more pleasant to be around now.

After almost two and a half years of consulting and having the freedom and flexibility I craved, I discovered that I underestimated how lonely consulting can feel.

Some days, the only people I talk to are the cashier where I pick up my coffee or my client, who only had time to discuss projects with me. Since I charged by the hour, we didn't have time for social chats. Being a consultant was a transactional working relationship, which made me realize that I missed being part of a team and missed leading a team.

I made the decision to give up my consulting business.

I began interviewing to go back in-house as an HR leader again. I interviewed, and I was very crisp on what I wanted because I knew what I needed, finally. I needed the following three pillars to sustain me in the long run:

---

41 Amy Morin, "What Are the Signs of a Midlife Crisis?" Verywell, November 24, 2020.

1. A good leadership team that is experienced or at least held other leadership positions previously;
2. A company that is doing something purposeful in the world; and
3. A company that has an appetite for elevating the role of HR to tackle the bigger problems of the future of work.

CHAPTER 15

MY SECOND ACT

In February of 2020, a deadly virus shuttered the world. COVID-19 hit while I was in the final stages of writing this book. The world of work has changed completely, with most offices closing their doors and sending their employees home to connect virtually. Most of us have had to work remotely from home for more than a year to contain this worldwide health crisis. All sorts of virtual technologies were deployed in rapid succession for every company on earth: Most meetings have turned into Google Hangouts, Microsoft Teams, or Zoom calls. If I was lonely before COVID, my feelings of isolation were exacerbated through this pandemic.

As I began to look for work, my interviews took place via virtual platforms except one where I met the CEO for coffee, taking a walk and wearing masks for fear of spreading this awful virus. It was strange walking and talking amidst a deadly pandemic ravaging the world.

Life during COVID taught us that we could all work remotely and still be productive citizens. We had more time with family and friends during the day, although setting boundaries between the personal and the professional became one of the hardest juggling acts of our lives.

Even harder was the ability to find harmony with your personal interruptions; it was too easy to wake up and start working only to realize it was 3:00 p.m., and we still hadn't brushed our teeth. What to have for lunch or even how to use the bathroom between back-to-back Zoom meetings were part of our steep learning curve. Zoom video meetings with cameras turned on allowed everyone access to their coworker's private homes, finally allowing us to see each other as real humans for what seemed like the first time.

In the early days of the pandemic, parents, pets, and kids were recurring characters in the backgrounds of work calls as many cities required residents to shelter in place to control the spread of the virus until a vaccine arrived. We were actually socially deprived by socially distancing from each other. Zoom calls with friends, family, and work colleagues became the only ways to engage in dialogues. Whole crops of newly invented software like Miro, a virtual whiteboard software, and Bramble, a virtual social platform, made it into our homes overnight.

The time that we stayed indoors balancing work and home life lasted longer than we expected, and we were all mentally drained. We all tried to make the most of it; we had no other choice. For me, after some soul-searching and some interviews, I got a full-time role back in-house.

In addition to the COVID-19 pandemic, the United States specifically had civic unrest and economic uncertainty throughout much of 2020 and 2021. It was a good time for me to be back in-house. HR teams were thrust into executive tables and board rooms like never before. We were no longer relegated to compliance, benefits, and office space: Instead, we were detailed operators, coaches, and strategists needed in the face of these intersecting crises. We were responsible for managing the people strategy of the business, which remains one of the most unpredictable pieces of the puzzle to maneuver.

I relished the chance to be back on a team and be part of a company again amidst all these pressures. With COVID mostly behind us, the burnout behind me, and this book written, I have a newfound energy to turn my focus to the future of work. I am still fighting to be an extraordinary person who builds great companies. I'm happy to be back in-house as an HR leader, and this time, it's going to be my greatest second act!

CHAPTER 16

HOPES FOR THE FUTURE

———

While it took me many years and attempts to find the right company and tribe, once I found it, I knew how to contribute my skills. The hard work of building a great workplace environment alongside the right tribe of colleagues was a recipe I desperately wanted to perfect. It took me many concoctions, and in the end, I had to face some adversity (abuse, tough conversations, and burnout to name a few) in order to find the secret sauce.

Looking back, I had the chance to build teams, systems, and operational flows for every tech company I worked at. I got the chance to lead the people side of an IPO transaction, completed seven different M&As, and handled a divestiture, among many other sophisticated transactions. I collected plenty of tools in my toolkit for working in all of these companies. As tech companies like to declare, you have to build the metaphorical plane while it's flying in the air. Many companies must innovate or they will become irrelevant in this day and age.[42]

---

42 Steve Little, "Building the Plane While Flying," *The Disruption Lab (blog)*, *January 22, 2020.*

Tech start-ups allowed me to learn and grow each day. The variety of tasks and projects and the constant firefighting while trying to plan for the next six months created a constant juggle of priorities. I love the thrill of being able to create, design, and launch all sorts of people programs. It is honestly what I thrive on the most; the idea that I can invent a new way of doing something, try it out, and revisit it when necessary energizes my batteries constantly. It's what has kept me on a high for most of my working life. I hope the ethos of relentless disruption continues to be one of the hallmarks of working in tech for many generations to come.

In order to tie all of the work streams together in a tech company, teams must create goals. Most companies plot goals each quarter. We called them objectives and key results, or OKRs, in most of the companies where I worked. Each quarter we would painstakingly commit to realistic goals along with unreasonable stretch goals forcing us to push our own boundaries. That was the charm of setting stretch goals: They dared all of us to dream a little bigger.

The crushing blow always came at the end of the quarter when you realize you've worked so hard but still ended up short of your own goals. Try this for eight straight quarters, and your life starts to look a little disappointing. *What the hell am I working so hard to accomplish?* might roam into your headspace, but the option of setting attainable goals isn't the style or vibe of working in a tech start-up either. Leaders in tech start-ups don't like when you aren't ambitious with your own goals. They want to push you out of your own comfort zone to accomplish more. I learned quickly that I had to dream bigger or be chided by my very own colleagues for not daring enough.

The strange pull of setting some goals beyond my reach and being disappointed every quarter seems like a distant memory looking back. I never felt bad for too long; I had too much to do to sit and wallow. As each quarter ended, I simply picked back up where we started and knew we had more time to try again. It can be exhausting and exhilarating at the same time. That's the thing about working in tech: You can love it and hate it at the same time. Somehow, I kept joining teams to run the drill all over again, learning more about my own grit and resilience each time. I was either insane or a glutton; on certain days, the line between the two was a tightrope. We all learn from failures, and we all regret not trying things; working in a tech company allows you to do both. I hope this remains a staple of why anyone would join a tech company.

Finally, and most dear to my heart, is the ability for tech to solve the diversity problem every company seems to talk about. Tech needs more diverse people in order to see all sides of a problem. The more viewpoints that exist on a team, the more likely you will solve the *right* problem. Research by McKinsey & Company shows that diverse teams drive better business results.[43]

One of my favorite stories is the story of how YouTube launched mobile video uploads to their platform. When they started mobile uploads concept, they encouraged the public to upload videos to their platform. It was supposed to be easy, and it was, except some video submissions appeared upside down on the platform. The engineers could not duplicate the problem; they looked for bugs in their platform for months—and still, nothing. The reason they could not duplicate the

---

43 Vivian Hunt, Dennis Layton, and Sarah Prince, "Why Diversity Matters."

upside-down problem was related to the fact that 90 percent of the world is made up of right-handed people.[44] It wasn't until they hired their first left-handed engineer that they correctly identified the problem. Finally able to replicate the problem, they discovered that the videos that appeared upside down on the platform were mostly submitted by left-handed people. The problem had to do with the way southpaws hold a phone.[45] They would have never identified the problem if they would have never made their team more diverse—in this case, by hiring a left-handed engineer.

Think about that: It was a simple problem of right-handedness versus left-handedness. It had nothing to do with bugs, lines of code, or even the product. It was the ability to capitalize on human diversity, which was right in front of them, that led to their own breakthrough.

Tech can be one of the most collaborative spaces you will find. These types of companies will allow you to have the impact you want. I guarantee that you will feel the impact of the many contributions from your high-effort work. The hardest part is that you must find the right company that you believe in and work alongside the right tribe of colleagues who can bring out the best in you.

I usually get to meet a new hire on their first day on the job and see them on their last day of work at the company. I want to make sure that even when they become an alum, they can look back fondly on their journey and smile knowing that their hard work made an impact.

---

44 Linda Searing, "The Big Number: Lefties Make up about 10 Percent of the World," *The Washington Post, August 12, 2019.*

45 S. Buckley, "Unconscious Bias Is Why We Don't Have a Diverse Workplace, Says Google," engadget, September 25, 2014.

We've all traveled from different places to get on this shared journey that is known as work. I believe we can do wonderful things together for the generations that follow, including Generation Z, the one my daughter belongs to. We're on our way to bigger and bolder things already. I know I am.

ACKNOWLEDGMENTS

———

First, I'd like to thank my family for their support during this book-writing journey. To Peter, thank you for having a full time job AND doing the hard work of keeping our family healthy, happy, and loving while I spent hours trying to write and finalize this book. To my mother, Hien Nguyen, who gave me an "Asian F" and asked nonchalantly, "Why are you spending your time writing a book?" She motivates me in profound ways. To my brother, Quang Bao, who helped make this book come to life. To my father, Pho Vinh, who I saw read every day of his life.

Thank you to all the people who contributed to this book. The people who I interviewed: Myra, Daniel Morris, Odette Lindheim, Melanie Oberman, Melissa, Priya Ollapally Wellington, Erin Grau, Ciara, and Brittany Brown Ceres. The people who were my beta readers: Stephanie Fogle, Samantha Price, Vanessa Kirby, Rin Chon, Melanie Oberman, Ciara Lakhani, Melissa Lightbody, Erin Grau, Hetal Patel, Myra Zheng, and Odette Lindheim. The people who wrote praise for my book: Alana Karen, Christine Tao, Cindy Owyoung, Lars Schmidt, Ed Frauenheim, and George LaRocque. Thank you for all the hours you spent with me over these past months. Your time was valuable to me, and I hope I captured the stories from your interviews and feedback. Thank you to the many people who gave me the stories on which to base this book. I worked with many of you and appreciate your trust in allowing me to tell your stories without naming names.

Thank you to my two coaches, Rajkumari Neogy and Christine Sachs, who helped me to create my own goals and dreams and make them happen.

Thank you to all the folks at New Degree Press: Professor Eric Koester, Kyrsten Rice, Bianca daSilva, Julie Colvin, Emma Colvin, Leila Summers, Gjorgji Pejkovsky, Brian Bies, Solaja Slobadan, Amanda Brown, Mary Hanna, and the many others who held my hand on this path to becoming an author.

Thank you to all my backers on Kickstarter. With your financial help, I was able to produce my first book with professionally trained writers who appear on this one page alone. Tan Nguyen, Lien Nguyen, Nam Nguyen, Chau Bao, Cindy Bao, Ngoc Bao, Peter Pai, Natalie Nguyen, Juliet Nguyen, Emma Pai, Christopher Forbes, Alexander Austin, Ju Rhyu, Rin Chon, Matthew Monahan, Sheryl Nicol, Samantha Low, Yimin Ge, Lesa Mellis, Andrew S Lee, Meagan Soszynski, Christine Sachs, William Growney, Thach Nguyen, Grace Chen, Marc Hayem, Brittany Ceres, Nono Yerbinis, Joanna Martin, Connor Swofford, Myra Zheng, Deniqua Crichlow, Christine Tao, Michael Dekshenieks, Brian Higgins, Cindy Owyoung, Zaina Orbai, Tharun Tej Tammineni, Stacy Proctor, Robert Marx, Joris Luijke, Taro Kodama, Christine Kung, Paul Callaghan, Didier Elzinga, Melanie Oberman, James Biernat, Erin Grau, Adrienne Cooper, May Lynn Tan, George C. Wu, Jeremy Liew, Iris Woo, Nikki Senaratne, Ronda

Atencion, Samantha Price, Dina Friedel, Deb Josephs, Allison Williams, Marjorie Ajero, Connie Poshala, Dornan McGuire, Nicola Porter-Smith, Michael Manne, Melissa Enbar, Rahim Lakhani, Joseph Yeh, Cindy Georgette, Mamuna Oyofo, Matt Gallatin, Jennifer Wilson, George LaRocque, John Dorning, Brittany Mullings, Caroline Gasparini, Anna Ivy, Odette Lindheim, Gina Lau, Sarah Bierenbaum, Jami Darwin Chiang, Katharine Bailey, Russell Elliot, Sarah Ruxin, Leslie Borrell, Dawn Childs, James Sumortin, Emma Leeds Guidarelli, Ellie Yuan, Paula Davidson, Laura Okawa , Lily Thau, Daniel Morris, Sunny Bates, Tammy San, Matt Barrio, Rajkumari Neogy, Florian Adolph, Kristine Joe, Linda Paul, Dwight Lee, Ciara Lakhani, William Potter, Rachel Zisser, Rebecca Scharfstein, Hillary Frank, Michele Li, Christopher Flores, Amy Knapp, Kristen Forti, Lars Schmidt, Abhilash Pillai, Jay Hanlon, Julie Li Melissa Lightbody, Laura Sue D'Annunzio, Bessie Chan, Sheila Long, Yasmin Nelson, Wolf Owczarek, Tieg Zaharia, Elyse Mallouk, Sean Leow, Amanda Niu, Craig Churchill, Alana Karen, Jane Veeder, Ann Quinn, Kate Bernyk, Jonathan Ritter-Roderick, Jon Leland, Lisa Looye, Emily Bunin, Luke Thomas, Bethany Crystal, Jeanna Cavanaugh, Terry Ruth VanDuyn, Eli Horne, Dan Smolkin, Anna Krasniewska, Sarah Walker, Deborah Lee, Drika Weller, Ed Frauenheim, Traci Nelson, Jess Galica, Maureen Edmonds, Kalyani Gopal, Shebani Patel, Jason Kaplan, Terry Venz, Lee Taylor, Stephanie Chace, Aziz Hasan, Fred Wilson, and The Creative Fund by BackerKit.

Finally, to my daughter, Emma: You inspire me because you simply ask questions to learn about the world around you. I work hard to show you that we can make our mark on the world together. Thank you for writing the forward for this book. I am proud that you get a slot in a book about work at the age of twelve! Mommy's job is to open doors for you sometimes; every once in a while, open your own door.

APPENDIX

INTRODUCTION

Woo, Jong-Min and Teodor T. Postolache. "The Impact of Work
Environment on Mood Disorders and Suicide: Evidence and
Implications." *International Journal on Disability and Human
Development* 7, no. 2 (2008): 185-200. https://doi.org/10.1515/
IJDHD.2008.7.2.185.

CHAPTER 1: BEGINNINGS

Urban Institute. "State and Local Finance Initiative." 2011. https://
www.urban.org/policy-centers/cross-center-initiatives/
state-and-local-finance-initiative/state-and-local-background-
ers/public-welfare-expenditures.

USA.gov. "Government Benefits." Accessed February 21, 2021.
https://www.usa.gov/benefits.

Young, Jeffery R. "How Many Times Will People Change Jobs? The
Myth of the Endlessly-Job-Hopping Millennial." EdSurge, July
20, 2017. https://www.edsurge.com/news/2017-07-20-how-ma-

APPENDIX · 171

ny-times-will-people-change-jobs-the-myth-of-the-endlessly-job-hopping-millennial.

CHAPTER 2: WHERE WAS HR?

Fowler, Susan. "Reflecting on One Very, Very Strange Year at Uber." *Susan Fowler* (blog). February 19, 2017. https://www.susanjfowler.com/blog/2017/2/19/reflecting-on-one-very-strange-year-at-uber.

Kim, Larry. "Building a Great Startup Culture Starts with the Founder." Medium. December 20, 2016. https://medium.com/the-mission/building-a-great-startup-culture-starts-with-the-founder-9d680e1198f1.

Meinert, Dori. "How to Investigate Sexual Harassment Allegations." *HR Magazine*, January 8, 2018. https://www.shrm.org/hr-today/news/hr-magazine/0218/pages/how-to-investigate-sexual-harassment-allegations.aspx.

Wolfe, Michael. "The Three Ways to Make a Lot of Money at a Startup." *Forbes*, October 31, 2013. https://www.forbes.com/sites/quora/2013/10/31/the-three-ways-to-make-a-lot-of-money-at-a-startup/?sh=7350a77260b2.

CHAPTER 5: MEDITATION & PING-PONG TABLES

Mohdin, Aamna. "If Ping-Pong Table Sales Are Falling, Then Silicon Valley Is Clearly Doomed." *Quartz*, May 4, 2016. https://qz.com/676050/if-ping-pong-table-sales-are-falling-then-silicon-valley-is-clearly-doomed/.

Newport, Cal. *Deep Work: Rules for Focused Success in a Distracted World*. New York: Grand Central Publishing, 2016.

CHAPTER 7: BURPING, FARTING, AND OTHER NOISES

Schwab, Katharine. "Everyone Hates Open Offices. Here's Why They Still Exist." *Fast Company*, January 15, 2019. https://www.fastcompany.com/90285582/everyone-hates-open-plan-offices-heres-why-they-still-exist.

CHAPTER 8: ON BEING A WOMAN IN TECH

Croswell, Alexis. "What Is Employee Engagement?" *Culture Amp* (blog). Accessed February 24, 2021. https://www.cultureamp.com/blog/what-is-employee-engagement/.

Haas, Susan Biali. "Forget Those Long Hours: Self-Care Drives Success." *Psychology Today*. September 19, 2018. https://www.psychologytoday.com/ca/blog/prescriptions-life/201809/forget-those-long-hours-self-care-drives-success.

Harter, Jim. "U.S. Employee Engagement Hits New High after Historic Drop." Gallup, July, 22, 2021. https://www.gallup.com/workplace/316064/employee-engagement-hits-new-high-historic-drop.aspx.

Hunt, Vivian, Dennis Layton, and Sarah Prince. "Why Diversity Matters." McKinsey & Company. January 1, 2015. https://www.mckinsey.com/business-functions/organization/our-insights/why-diversity-matters.

Wong, Kelly. "10 Shocking Stats on Employee Disengagement." *Achievers* (blog). July 9, 2019. https://www.achievers.com/blog/10-shocking-stats-on-employee-disengagement/.

Yoshimoto, Catherine and Ed Frauenheim. "The Best Companies to Work for Are Beating the Market." *Fortune*, February 27, 2018. https://fortune.com/2018/02/27/the-best-companies-to-work-for-are-beating-the-market/.

CHAPTER 9: ON PERKS AND PRIVILEGES

Barrie, Leslie. "Wellness Perks Aren't Just a Draw for Silicon Valley Jobs Anymore." Skift, March 28, 2019. https://skift.com/2019/03/28/wellness-perks-arent-just-a-draw-for-silicon-valley-jobs-anymore/.

Parris, Richard. "20 Best Companies for Employee Benefits and Perks." Tech.co, May 13, 2020. https://tech.co/performance-management-software/best-companies-employee-perks-benefits.

Reinberg, Steven. "Could Your Office Job Rob You of Vitamin D?" Medical Xpress, June 22, 2017. https://medicalxpress.com/news/2017-06-office-job-vitamin-d.html.

Schrodt, Paul. "12 Companies with the Most Luxurious Employee Perks." *Money*, October 9, 2017. https://money.com/12-companies-with-the-most-luxurious-employee-perks/.

CHAPTER 10: JIMMY CHOOS

Blank, Steve. "Organizational Debt Is like Technical Debt—but Worse." *Steve Blank* (blog). May 19, 2015. https://steveblank. com/2015/05/19/organizational-debt-is-like-technical-debt-but-worse/.

CHAPTER 11: CONTINUOUS LEARNING

Clapon, Paula. "Can the Tech Industry Solve the Employee Tenure Problem?." Hppy. Accessed on February 9, 2021. https://gethppy. com/employee-engagement/can-tech-industry-solve-employee-tenure-problem.

CHAPTER 12: ON WORKING WITH MILLENNIALS

Fry, Richard. "Millennials Are the Largest Generation in the U.S. Labor Force." Pew Research Center. April 11, 2018. https://www. pewresearch.org/fact-tank/2018/04/11/millennials-largest-generation-us-labor-force/.

Kaiser, Caleb. "How to Hire Your First 10 Employees." *AngelList Blog*. August 17, 2018. https://angel.co/blog/how-to-hire-your-first-10-employees.

Paychex. "How to Manage the 5 Generations in the Workplace." Last modified July 26, 2019. https://www.paychex.com/articles/human-resources/how-to-manage-multiple-generations-in-the-workplace.

Pollak, Lindsey. "Gen X, the Forgotten Middle Child: Is It Any Wonder That Our Theme Song Is 'Don't You Forget about Me?'" *Lindsey Pollock* (blog). September 9, 2019. https://lindseypollak.

com/gen-x-the-forgotten-middle-child-is-it-any-wonder-that-our-theme-song-is-dont-you-forget-about-me/.

CHAPTER 13: BURNOUT

Booz, Michael. "These 3 Industries Have the Highest Talent Turnover Rates." *Linkedin Talent Blog.* March 15, 2018. https://business.linkedin.com/talent-solutions/blog/trends-and-research/2018/the-3-industries-with-the-highest-turnover-rates.

Clapon, Paula. "Can the Tech Industry Solve the Employee Tenure Problem?" Hppy, Accessed on February 9, 2021. https://gethppy.com/employee-engagement/can-tech-industry-solve-employee-tenure-problem.

Ton, Mai. "Burn(ed) out." Medium. October 7, 2019. https://medium.com/@maitonpai_18792/burn-ed-out-f182957ab93d.

Ton, Mai and Lars Schmidt. "Ep39 EMP HR Consulting Founder Mai Ton, Navigating Burnout in HR." November 11th, 2019. In *21st Century HR.* Produced by Lars Schmidt. Podcast, MP3 audio, 24:18. https://21stcenturyhr.fireside.fm/ep39-emp-hr-consulting-founder-mai-ton-navigating-burnout-in-hr.

World Health Organization. "Burn-Out an 'Occupational Phenomenon': International Classification of Diseases." May 28, 2019. https://www.who.int/news/item/28-05-2019-burn-out-an-occupational-phenomenon-international-classification-of-diseases.

World Health Organization. "Occupational Health: Stress at the Workplace." Q&A Detail. October 19, 2020. https://www.who.

int/news-room/q-a-detail/ccupational-health-stress-at-the-workplace.

CHAPTER 14: CONSULTING

McCallum, Dena, Susan J. Ashford, and Brianna Barker Caza. "Why Consultants Quit Their Jobs to Go Independent." *Harvard Business Review*, July 15, 2019. https://hbr.org/2019/07/why-consultants-quit-their-jobs-to-go-independent.

Morin, Amy. "What Are the Signs of a Midlife Crisis?" Verywell, November 24, 2020. https://www.verywellmind.com/what-are-the-signs-of-a-midlife-crisis-4175827.

CHAPTER 16: HOPES FOR THE FUTURE

Buckley, S. "Unconscious Bias Is Why We Don't Have a Diverse Workplace, Says Google." engadget, September 25, 2014. https://www.engadget.com/2014-09-25-unconscious-bias-is-why-we-dont-have-a-diverse-workplace-says.html.

Hunt, Vivian, Dennis Layton, and Sarah Prince. "Why Diversity Matters." McKinsey & Company. January 1, 2015. https://www.mckinsey.com/business-functions/organization/our-insights/why-diversity-matters.

Little, Steve. "Building the Plane While Flying." *The Disruption Lab* (blog). January 22, 2020. https://thedisruptionlab.com/building-the-plane-while-flying/.

Searing, Linda. "The Big Number: Lefties Make up about 10 Percent of the World." *The Washington Post*, August 12, 2019. https://

www.washingtonpost.com/health/the-big-number-lefties-make-up-about-10-percent-of-the-world/2019/08/09/69978100-b9e2-11e9-bad6-609f75bfd97f_story.html.

Made in the USA
Las Vegas, NV
24 May 2021

23610192R00098